HOW TO SPEAK WELL

A Practical Guide to Becoming a Well-Articulated Confident Speaker

JAMIE RAMSEY

Copyright Notice

This book is copyrighted in 2019-2022 by Dan & Elbert Associates.

All rights reserved.
Its content may not be copied or duplicated in part or whole by any means without express prior agreement in writing

TABLE OF CONTENTS

Introduction   5
Chapter 1: Understanding the Power of Speech   7
    1.1 The Impact of Clear Communication   7
    1.2 Identifying Personal Speech Challenges   9
    1.3 Setting Clear Communication Goals   11
Chapter 2: The Importance of Confidence   15
    2.1 Exploring the Link Between Confidence and Speech   15
    2.2 Building Confidence through Self-Awareness   17
    2.3 Adopting Confidence-Building Practices   20
Chapter 3: Mastering Pronunciation   25
    3.1 Understanding the Role of Pronunciation in Clarity   25
    3.2 Practicing Pronunciation Techniques   27
    3.3 Seeking Feedback on Pronunciation   32
Chapter 4: Breathing and Vocal Exercises   35
    4.1 The Importance of Breath Control In Speech   35
    4.2 Vocal Warm-Up Routines   37
    4.3 Incorporating Vocal Dynamics   39
Chapter 5: Pace and Pauses   43
    5.1 Recognizing the Impact of Pace and Pauses   43
    5.2 Adjusting Pace for Effective Communication   47
    5.3 Harnessing the Power of Strategic Pauses   48
Chapter 6: Listening Skills   53
    6.1 Developing Active Listening Habits   53
    6.2 Improving Listening Comprehension   57

6.3 Providing Constructive Feedback	59
Chapter 7: Overcoming Fear of Public Speaking	**63**
7.1 Understanding the Roots of Public Speaking Anxiety	63
7.2 Building Confidence through Preparation	70
7.3 Gradual Exposure to Public Speaking	72
Chapter 8: Building Vocabulary and Language Skills	**77**
8.1 Expanding Your Vocabulary	77
8.2 Using Language in Context	79
8.3 Exploring Language Through Reading	80
Chapter 9: Practicing Regularly	**83**
9.1 Making Speech Practice a Habit	83
9.2 Incorporating Feedback Loops	84
9.3 Applying Skills in Real-Life Situations	85
Chapter 10: Seeking Feedback and Improvement	**87**
10.1 Embracing Constructive Criticism	87
10.2 Utilizing Feedback for Continuous Improvement	88
10.3 Self-Assessment and Reflection	90
Chapter 11: Embracing Your Unique Voice	**93**
11.1 Celebrating Individuality in Speech	93
11.2 Cultivating Confidence in Your Voice	94
11.3 Finding Your Speaking Persona	96
Conclusion - A Journey of Healing	**99**

Introduction

Picture this: You stand before a crowd, your words hanging in the air with a clarity that commands attention. Every syllable you utter resonates with confidence, leaving your audience captivated by the power of your speech. Sounds like a scene from a distant dream, doesn't it? But what if I told you that dream could be your reality?

Welcome to "How to Speak Well," where we're about to embark on a transformative journey—one that will unlock the hidden potential of your voice. Whether you're a timid speaker struggling to be heard or an eloquent communicator seeking to refine your skills, this book is your roadmap to speaking with clarity, conviction, and charisma.

Think of this as your personal crash course in communication excellence. Each chapter is carefully crafted to provide you with actionable insights, practical exercises, and expert tips to help you master the art of effective speech. From conquering pronunciation hurdles to banishing public speaking jitters, we'll cover it all and more.

But this isn't just about mastering vocal techniques. It's about uncovering the power within you to express yourself with authenticity and impact. It's about embracing your unique voice, celebrating your individuality, and leaving a lasting impression with every word you speak.

So, are you ready to embark on this exhilarating journey? If you're willing to roll up your sleeves, dive in headfirst, and commit to unleashing the full potential of your voice, then let's get started. The stage is set, and the spotlight is waiting for you. It's time to become the articulate, confident speaker you were always meant to be.

Chapter 1:
Understanding the Power of Speech

Speech is a fundamental aspect of human communication, serving as a powerful tool for conveying thoughts, ideas, and emotions. From casual conversations to formal presentations, the clarity and effectiveness of our speech can significantly impact the way we interact with others and the impression we leave behind. In this chapter, we will delve into the importance of clear communication, explore common speech challenges, and establish clear communication goals to enhance speech clarity and confidence.

1.1 The Impact of Clear Communication

Clear communication is the cornerstone of effective human interaction, serving as a vital conduit for fostering understanding, building relationships, and achieving shared goals. When our speech lacks clarity or becomes muddled, it can sow the seeds of confusion, misunderstandings, and frustration, hindering our ability to connect with others and collaborate effectively. Consider a scenario where miscommunication occurs in a recent conversation, illustrating the profound consequences of unclear speech.

Imagine you're tasked with discussing a critical project with a colleague. As you engage in conversation, you find yourself struggling to articulate your ideas clearly, leading to vague instructions and ambiguous expectations. Consequently, your colleague is left feeling perplexed, unsure of what is required and when it needs to be completed. The result? Confusion reigns, deadlines are missed, and frustration mounts on both sides.

Now, pause for a moment and reflect on how clarity in speech could have transformed this scenario. What if you had taken the time to articulate your thoughts with precision, providing clear and concise instructions to your colleague? By communicating expectations explicitly and outlining a detailed plan of action, you could have eliminated ambiguity and empowered your colleague to execute their tasks effectively. Instead of floundering in uncertainty, both parties would have been aligned in their understanding, fostering a sense of clarity and purpose in their collaboration.

Analyzing past instances of miscommunication allows us to glean valuable insights into the importance of clarity in speech and its profound impact on interpersonal interactions. By dissecting the root causes of communication breakdowns, we can uncover patterns of ambiguity, inconsistency, or misunderstanding that hinder effective dialogue. Armed with this awareness, we can take proactive steps to enhance our communication skills, ensuring that our messages are conveyed with clarity, coherence, and conviction.

Indeed, the ability to communicate clearly is not merely a desirable trait but an essential skill for navigating the complexities of the modern world. Whether in the boardroom, the classroom, or the living room, clear communication lays the foundation for meaningful connections, productive collaborations, and successful outcomes. By prioritizing clarity in speech and striving for precision in our communication, we can transcend barriers, bridge divides, and forge stronger bonds with those around us.

Action Task: Reflect on a recent conversation where miscommunication occurred. Identify how clarity in speech could have improved understanding. Consider factors such as tone, language choice, and nonverbal cues. Write down your observations and consider how you can apply them to future communication scenarios.

1.2 Identifying Personal Speech Challenges

Each of us possesses a distinct set of speech patterns and habits that shape the way we communicate with others. These idiosyncrasies, whether they stem from regional dialects, cultural influences, or individual quirks, play a significant role in determining the clarity and effectiveness of our speech. However, not all speech patterns are created equal, and some may inadvertently hinder our ability to convey our thoughts and ideas with precision and confidence.

Identifying personal speech challenges is the crucial first step toward improving speech clarity and confidence. By taking a moment to reflect on situations where we feel most challenged in speaking clearly, we can begin to unravel the complexities of our communication style and uncover areas for improvement.

Consider the environments in which you often find yourself struggling to make yourself heard. Are noisy settings, such as crowded cafes or bustling streets, a frequent source of frustration? In these cacophonous environments, background noise can drown out our words, making it difficult for others to discern what we're saying. As a result, we may find ourselves repeating statements or raising our voices in an attempt to be heard, only to further exacerbate the problem.

Similarly, large group discussions or meetings can pose a unique set of challenges for those with speech difficulties. In these settings, the pressure to assert oneself and contribute to the conversation can trigger feelings of anxiety or self-doubt, leading to hesitancy or reluctance to speak up. As a result, valuable insights may go unshared, and opportunities for meaningful contribution may be missed.

Furthermore, consider how your speech patterns may be influenced by emotional states such as nervousness or anxiety. Do you find yourself stumbling over words or speaking too quickly when faced with stressful situations? These physiological responses to stress can manifest in verbal communication, causing us to fumble our words or rush through sentences in an effort to alleviate discomfort. However, this haste often leads to decreased clarity and comprehension, as our words become jumbled and our message gets lost in the fray.

By pinpointing these challenges and reflecting on the underlying factors contributing to speech difficulties, we can gain a deeper understanding of our communication patterns and their impact on our interactions with others. Armed with this awareness, we can begin to develop strategies for overcoming speech obstacles and cultivating greater clarity and confidence in our communication.

In the following chapters, we will explore practical techniques and exercises designed to address common speech challenges and enhance speech clarity and confidence. From mastering pronunciation and enunciation to building confidence and overcoming anxiety, each chapter will provide valuable insights and actionable strategies to help you unlock the full potential of your voice. So, take the time to reflect on your own speech challenges, and let's embark on this journey toward improved communication together.

Action Task: List situations where you feel most challenged in speaking clearly. Analyze common factors contributing to these challenges, such as environmental distractions, anxiety, or lack of preparation. Consider how these challenges impact your ability to communicate effectively and brainstorm strategies for overcoming them.

1.3 Setting Clear Communication Goals

Setting clear communication goals is a fundamental aspect of improving speech clarity and confidence. Whether you're aiming to speak more confidently in public settings, articulate your thoughts more clearly in conversations, or reduce instances of mumbling or stuttering, establishing specific goals provides a roadmap for achieving lasting improvement in your communication skills.

To begin, it's essential to take the time to identify areas where you would like to enhance your communication skills. Reflect on past experiences and interactions where you felt your speech lacked clarity or confidence. Are there particular situations or contexts in which you struggle to effectively convey your message? Perhaps you've noticed recurring patterns of speech difficulties, such as mumbling, stuttering, or difficulty organizing your thoughts coherently.

Once you've identified areas for improvement, the next step is to establish concrete objectives for achieving your communication goals. These objectives should be specific, measurable, achievable, relevant, and time-bound (SMART). For example, if your goal is to speak more confidently in public settings, you might set an objective to deliver a five-minute speech at a local community event within the next three months.

After defining your goals, it's crucial to create a plan outlining actionable steps you can take to reach them. Break down each goal into smaller, manageable tasks that you can work on consistently over time. For instance, if your goal is to articulate your thoughts more clearly in conversations, some actionable steps might include:

1. Practice active listening during conversations to ensure you understand others' perspectives and respond appropriately.

2. Focus on speaking slowly and deliberately, enunciating each word clearly to enhance clarity.
3. Incorporate vocabulary-building exercises into your daily routine to expand your language skills and express yourself more effectively.
4. Seek opportunities to engage in meaningful conversations with friends, family members, or colleagues, actively seeking feedback on your communication skills.

By breaking down your goals into actionable steps, you can create a roadmap for success and track your progress over time. Additionally, writing down your goals and plan can help solidify your commitment to improving your communication skills and provide a tangible reference point for staying on track.

Setting clear communication goals is essential for improving speech clarity and confidence. By identifying areas for improvement, establishing specific objectives, and creating a plan outlining actionable steps, you can take proactive steps toward achieving lasting improvement in your communication skills. So, take the time to define your goals, create a plan, and embark on the journey toward enhanced communication with confidence and clarity.

Action Task: Establish specific goals for improving your speech clarity and confidence. Consider areas such as pronunciation, pacing, vocal projection, and nonverbal communication. Write them down and create a plan to achieve them, breaking down larger goals into smaller, manageable tasks. Set deadlines for each task and track your progress regularly to stay motivated and accountable.

By understanding the impact of clear communication, identifying personal speech challenges, and setting clear communication goals, we lay the foundation for improving speech clarity and confidence. In the following chapters, we will explore practical techniques and exercises to help you overcome speech obstacles and unleash the full potential of your voice.

Chapter 2:
The Importance of Confidence

Confidence is not just a state of mind; it's a powerful catalyst that shapes our actions, influences our interactions, and ultimately determines our success in life. In the realm of communication, confidence plays a pivotal role in our ability to express ourselves effectively, connect with others, and leave a lasting impression. In this chapter, we will explore the intrinsic link between confidence and speech, delve into strategies for building confidence through self-awareness, and adopt confidence-building practices to unlock our full potential as communicators.

2.1 Exploring the Link Between Confidence and Speech

Confidence and effective communication share a symbiotic relationship that significantly influences our ability to express ourselves with clarity and conviction. This intricate connection between confidence and speech is deeply rooted in psychological principles and has been extensively studied to uncover its profound impact on our communication abilities.

Research into the connection between confidence and speech has yielded compelling insights into the ways in which self-assurance shapes our communication effectiveness. Numerous studies have demonstrated a positive correlation between confidence and perceived competence in communication. Individuals who exude confidence in their speech are not only perceived as more credible and persuasive but also as more authoritative, leading to greater influence and impact in their interactions with others.

For instance, a study conducted by researchers at Stanford University found that speakers who exhibited confident body language, such as maintaining eye contact, using expressive gestures, and standing tall, were perceived as more persuasive and trustworthy by their audience. These findings underscore the powerful influence that confidence exerts on listener perceptions and highlight the importance of nonverbal cues in shaping our communication effectiveness

Moreover, confidence is contagious, with its effects extending beyond the individual to influence the dynamics of interpersonal interactions. When we speak with confidence, we inspire trust and admiration in those who witness it, thereby enhancing the effectiveness of our communication efforts. This phenomenon, known as the "confidence cascade," occurs when the confidence of one individual influences the confidence levels of others, creating a positive feedback loop that elevates the overall quality of communication within a group or team.

In a study published in the Journal of Personality and Social Psychology, researchers found that individuals who were exposed to confident speakers were more likely to exhibit confidence themselves in subsequent interactions. This ripple effect of confidence not only enhances the receptivity of listeners but also fosters a collaborative atmosphere where ideas can be freely exchanged and explored.

Furthermore, confidence serves as a catalyst for assertiveness and assertive communication, enabling individuals to express their thoughts, ideas, and emotions with clarity and conviction. Assertive communication is characterized by a balance between expressing one's own needs and respecting the needs of others, fostering open dialogue and mutual understanding.

In contrast, individuals who lack confidence may struggle to assert themselves effectively, leading to passive or passive-aggressive communication styles that hinder genuine connection and collaboration. By cultivating confidence in their speech, individuals can break free from the constraints of self-doubt and insecurity, empowering themselves to communicate assertively and authentically.

The link between confidence and effective communication is undeniable, with each reinforcing the other in a symbiotic relationship that fuels our ability to convey our thoughts, ideas, and emotions with clarity and conviction. Through research and empirical evidence, we gain valuable insights into the profound impact that self-assurance can have on our communication abilities, inspiring trust, admiration, and collaboration in those who witness it. By cultivating confidence in our speech, we unlock the full potential of our communication skills and pave the way for greater success and fulfillment in both personal and professional contexts.

2.2 Building Confidence through Self-Awareness

Self-awareness lies at the heart of confidence, serving as the foundation upon which we can cultivate a positive self-image and belief in our abilities. It is the ability to recognize and understand our thoughts, emotions, and behaviors, allowing us to navigate the world with clarity and authenticity. Yet, despite its importance, self-awareness is often overlooked or neglected in our quest for confidence and success.

All too often, negative self-talk and limiting beliefs can erode our confidence and undermine our communication efforts. These internal barriers, born from a lack of self-awareness, can manifest as doubts, fears, and self-critical thoughts that chip away at our self-esteem and inhibit our ability to express ourselves authentically.

Consider, for a moment, your own inner dialogue related to your speaking abilities. When preparing for a presentation or engaging in conversation, do you find yourself plagued by doubts about your competence or fears of being judged by others? Do you succumb to self-critical thoughts that undermine your confidence and leave you feeling inadequate?

These negative narratives are not merely harmless musings but powerful forces that shape our beliefs and behaviors. They act as barriers to our self-assurance, preventing us from fully embracing our potential and expressing ourselves authentically. However, by identifying and challenging these internal barriers, we can pave the way for greater self-assurance and empowerment in our speech.

The first step in this process is to cultivate self-awareness by tuning into our thoughts and emotions with curiosity and compassion. Take a moment to observe your inner dialogue related to your speaking abilities without judgment or criticism. Notice the patterns of negative self-talk and limiting beliefs that arise, and acknowledge their presence without giving them power over you.

Once you've identified these internal barriers, the next step is to challenge them with a spirit of curiosity and inquiry. Ask yourself: Are these thoughts based on objective reality, or are they distorted perceptions fueled by fear and insecurity? What evidence do I have to support these beliefs, and is there evidence to the contrary?

For example, if you find yourself doubting your ability to deliver a successful presentation, challenge this belief by recalling past successes or instances where you received positive feedback on your communication skills. Remind yourself of your strengths, skills, and achievements, and recognize that temporary setbacks do not define your worth or capabilities.

Moreover, cultivate a practice of self-compassion and kindness toward yourself, especially in moments of self-doubt or vulnerability. Treat yourself with the same warmth and understanding that you would offer to a close friend facing similar challenges. Remember that it's okay to make mistakes, stumble, and falter along the way—these are all part of the human experience.

In addition to challenging negative self-talk, actively cultivate a positive self-image and belief in your abilities. Affirmations are a powerful tool for rewiring your subconscious mind and reinforcing positive beliefs about yourself. Create affirmations that resonate with you and repeat them regularly to instill a sense of confidence and empowerment in your speech.

For example, affirmations such as "I am a confident and articulate communicator," "I trust in my ability to express myself clearly and effectively," or "I embrace challenges as opportunities for growth and learning" can help counteract negative self-talk and bolster your self-assurance.

Furthermore, seek out opportunities to expand your comfort zone and challenge yourself in areas where you feel less confident. Whether it's volunteering to speak at a meeting, joining a public speaking club, or enrolling in a communication skills workshop, stepping outside your comfort zone can help build resilience and confidence in your abilities.

Lastly, surround yourself with supportive individuals who uplift and encourage you on your journey toward greater self-assurance. Seek out mentors, coaches, or friends who believe in your potential and offer constructive feedback and encouragement. Their guidance and support can provide invaluable reassurance and validation as you navigate the ups and downs of building confidence in your speech.

In conclusion, self-awareness lies at the heart of confidence, serving as the foundation upon which we can cultivate a positive self-image and belief in our abilities. By identifying and challenging negative self-talk and limiting beliefs, we can pave the way for greater self-assurance and empowerment in our speech. Through practices such as self-compassion, positive affirmations, stepping outside our comfort zone, and seeking support from others, we can overcome internal barriers and unlock our full potential as confident and articulate communicators.

Action Task: Identify and challenge negative self-talk related to your speaking abilities. Keep a journal to record instances of self-doubt or criticism that arise in relation to your communication skills. Practice reframing these negative thoughts into positive affirmations that affirm your worth and capability as a communicator. Repeat these affirmations daily to reinforce a mindset of confidence and self-assurance.

2.3 Adopting Confidence-Building Practices

Confidence is often viewed as an elusive trait, possessed by a select few who seem to effortlessly command attention and assert themselves in any situation. However, contrary to popular belief, confidence is not an innate quality reserved for the lucky few but rather a skill that can be cultivated and strengthened through intentional practice and repetition. By adopting confidence-building practices into our daily routine, we can gradually expand our comfort zone, challenge our perceived limitations, and unlock our full potential as communicators.

One effective technique for building confidence is power posing, a concept popularized by social psychologist Amy Cuddy. Power poses involve assuming expansive, open body postures that convey confidence and dominance, such as standing tall with arms outstretched or hands on hips. These poses are designed to activate hormonal responses in the body, increasing levels of testosterone (associated with dominance and assertiveness) and decreasing levels of cortisol (associated with stress and anxiety).

Research conducted by Cuddy and her colleagues has shown that adopting power poses for just a few minutes can lead to significant increases in feelings of confidence and empowerment. In one study, participants who engaged in high-power poses before a job interview were more likely to be perceived as confident, competent, and hireable by interviewers compared to those who adopted low-power poses.

Action Task: Experiment with power poses in your daily routine. Set aside a few minutes each day to practice standing or sitting in a confident, expansive posture. Notice how adopting these poses affects your mood, demeanor, and sense of self-assurance. Over time, make power posing a regular part of your routine, incorporating it into your pre-presentation or pre-meeting rituals to boost your confidence and presence.

Visualization exercises are another powerful tool for building confidence. By mentally rehearsing successful communication scenarios in vivid detail, we can prime our minds and bodies to respond with confidence when faced with real-life situations. Picture yourself delivering a flawless presentation, engaging in a captivating conversation, or speaking with authority and conviction. As you visualize these scenarios, immerse yourself in the experience, tapping into the feelings of confidence and assurance that accompany them.

Action Task: Set aside time each day to practice visualization exercises. Find a quiet, comfortable space where you can relax and focus your mind. Close your eyes and imagine yourself in a specific communication scenario, such as giving a speech or participating in a meeting. Visualize the scene in as much detail as possible, imagining the sights, sounds, and sensations associated with success. Notice how you feel during the visualization process and take note of any areas where you can enhance your confidence and presence.

In addition to power posing and visualization exercises, there are several other strategies you can employ to build confidence in your communication skills:

1. Practice mindfulness: Mindfulness techniques, such as deep breathing and meditation, can help calm the mind and reduce feelings of anxiety and self-doubt. Incorporate mindfulness into your daily routine to cultivate a sense of inner calm and presence.

2. Set realistic goals: Break down larger communication goals into smaller, achievable tasks, and celebrate your progress along the way. Setting realistic goals allows you to build momentum and confidence as you work toward larger objectives.

3. Seek feedback: Actively seek feedback from trusted sources, such as mentors, peers, or colleagues, on your communication skills. Use constructive feedback as an opportunity for growth and improvement, and recognize that feedback is essential for building confidence and competence.

4. Embrace failure: Recognize that failure is a natural part of the learning process and an opportunity for growth. Instead of fearing failure, embrace it as a chance to learn from mistakes and refine your approach. By reframing failure as a stepping stone rather than a stumbling block, you can build resilience and confidence in your communication abilities.

By incorporating these confidence-building practices into your daily routine, you can gradually expand your comfort zone, challenge your perceived limitations, and unlock your full potential as a communicator. Remember that confidence is not a fixed attribute but a skill that can be cultivated and strengthened over time. With practice and persistence, you can build the confidence and presence needed to communicate with clarity, conviction, and authenticity.

Chapter 3:
Mastering Pronunciation

Pronunciation plays a pivotal role in the clarity and effectiveness of communication. Clear and accurate pronunciation ensures that our words are understood by others, facilitating meaningful interaction and conveying our intended message with precision. In this chapter, we will explore the importance of pronunciation in clarity, delve into practical techniques for mastering pronunciation, and discuss strategies for seeking feedback to refine our skills.

3.1 Understanding the Role of Pronunciation in Clarity

Pronunciation stands as the cornerstone of effective communication, wielding a profound influence on how our messages are perceived and comprehended by others. When our pronunciation is clear and accurate, it serves as a conduit through which our thoughts and ideas are conveyed with clarity and precision. Clear pronunciation enhances comprehension, enabling listeners to decipher words and phrases accurately and follow the flow of conversation effortlessly. Conversely, poor pronunciation can act as a barrier to understanding, leading to confusion, misunderstanding, and breakdowns in communication.

Imagine a scenario where you are engaged in conversation with someone whose pronunciation is muddled or unclear. Despite your best efforts to grasp their meaning, you find yourself struggling to decipher their words, leading to frustration and a sense of disconnect. In such instances, the lack of clear pronunciation hampers the flow of communication, impeding the exchange of ideas and inhibiting genuine understanding.

Clear pronunciation is especially crucial in multilingual or multicultural settings, where individuals may have varying levels of proficiency in the language being spoken. In these contexts, clear pronunciation serves as a bridge that facilitates communication across linguistic and cultural boundaries, enabling individuals to engage in meaningful dialogue and exchange ideas effectively.

Moreover, clear pronunciation fosters a sense of confidence and credibility in the speaker, enhancing their overall persuasiveness and authority. When we articulate our words clearly and confidently, we project an image of competence and professionalism, earning the trust and respect of our audience. In contrast, poor pronunciation can undermine our credibility and detract from the persuasiveness of our message, leading listeners to question our competence and authority.

In academic and professional settings, clear pronunciation is essential for conveying complex ideas and information accurately. Whether delivering a presentation, participating in a meeting, or engaging in a discussion, effective communication hinges on the ability to articulate words and phrases clearly and intelligibly. Clear pronunciation not only ensures that our message is understood correctly but also enhances our ability to engage and persuade our audience.

Furthermore, clear pronunciation is a sign of respect for our listeners, demonstrating our commitment to effective communication and mutual understanding. When we take the time to articulate our words clearly and accurately, we show consideration for the needs and preferences of our audience, fostering a positive and productive communication environment.

Pronunciation serves as the cornerstone of effective communication, influencing how our message is perceived and understood by others. Clear pronunciation enhances comprehension, enabling listeners to decipher words and phrases accurately and follow the flow of conversation effortlessly. Conversely, poor pronunciation can lead to confusion, misunderstanding, and breakdowns in communication. By prioritizing clear pronunciation in our communication efforts, we can enhance our ability to connect with others, convey our ideas effectively, and build stronger relationships in both personal and professional settings.

Action Task: To gain a deeper understanding of the role of pronunciation in clarity, listen to recordings of proficient speakers in your target language or dialect. Pay close attention to their pronunciation, noting the clarity and precision with which they articulate each sound. Observe how clear pronunciation contributes to overall comprehension and facilitates smooth communication. Take note of any specific techniques or strategies employed by proficient speakers to enhance clarity in their speech.

By analyzing the pronunciation of proficient speakers, we can gain valuable insights into the importance of clear articulation and enunciation in effective communication. These observations can inform our own pronunciation practice and help us identify areas for improvement in our speech.

3.2 Practicing Pronunciation Techniques

Mastering pronunciation is a journey that requires dedicated practice and attention to detail. It involves honing the ability to articulate sounds accurately and consistently, ensuring that our speech is clear and intelligible to others. By focusing on specific techniques and exercises, we can strengthen our pronunciation skills and overcome common challenges in speech. Tongue placement exercises, in particular, are a valuable tool for improving difficult sounds and enhancing overall clarity in pronunciation.

Tongue placement exercises target the muscles of the tongue and mouth, helping to develop greater control and coordination in articulating sounds. These exercises focus on manipulating the position of the tongue to produce specific sounds with precision and accuracy. By practicing tongue placement exercises regularly, we can train our articulatory muscles to produce sounds more effectively, leading to clearer and more accurate pronunciation.

One common challenge in pronunciation is mastering sounds that are not present in our native language or dialect. For example, English learners may struggle with sounds such as the "th" sound in words like "think" or the rolled "r" sound in languages like Spanish or Italian. Tongue placement exercises can help learners overcome these challenges by providing targeted practice for difficult sounds.

For example, to practice the "th" sound, learners can try placing the tip of their tongue between their upper and lower teeth, allowing air to flow through the gap to produce the sound. By repeating this exercise regularly, learners can train their tongue to position itself correctly and produce the sound accurately.

Similarly, for learners struggling with the rolled "r" sound, tongue placement exercises can help develop the necessary muscle control and coordination. One effective exercise involves rolling the tip of the tongue backward along the roof of the mouth while exhaling gently, producing a vibration that mimics the sound of the rolled "r." With consistent practice, learners can improve their ability to produce this challenging sound with greater clarity and precision.

In addition to targeting specific sounds, tongue placement exercises play a crucial role in improving overall clarity and articulation in pronunciation. These exercises not only focus on mastering individual sounds but also on developing the agility and flexibility of the tongue, allowing for smooth and precise movement between sounds. By enhancing tongue agility and flexibility, learners can reduce instances of slurred speech or unclear articulation, leading to clearer and more intelligible pronunciation.

One of the key benefits of tongue placement exercises that focus on agility and flexibility is their ability to improve the coordination and control of tongue movements. The tongue is a highly flexible muscle that plays a central role in shaping the sounds of speech. However, poor coordination or control of tongue movements can result in imprecise articulation and difficulty in producing certain sounds accurately.

By practicing exercises that target tongue agility and flexibility, learners can develop greater control over the movements of their tongue, allowing for more precise and controlled articulation of sounds. These exercises often involve a series of repetitive movements or gestures designed to strengthen the muscles of the tongue and improve coordination between different parts of the mouth.

For example, tongue trills are a popular exercise that can help improve tongue agility and coordination. To perform a tongue trill, learners can place the tip of their tongue against the roof of their mouth and rapidly vibrate it by exhaling air. This exercise helps to strengthen the muscles of the tongue and improve coordination between the tongue and the breath, leading to smoother and more controlled articulation of sounds.

Another effective exercise for improving tongue agility and flexibility is tongue twisters. Tongue twisters are phrases or sentences that contain a combination of sounds that are challenging to pronounce quickly and accurately. By repeating tongue twisters aloud at a moderate pace, learners can challenge themselves to move their tongue quickly and smoothly between sounds, improving their ability to articulate words clearly and accurately.

Aside from tongue trills and tongue twisters, numerous other exercises exist to enhance tongue agility and flexibility. Among these, tongue stretches and tongue push-ups stand out as effective methods to bolster the range of motion and strength of the tongue muscles, thereby refining pronunciation skills.

Tongue stretches aim to expand the tongue's flexibility by stretching it in various directions. To perform this exercise, begin by extending the tongue as far forward as possible, reaching towards the chin. Hold this position for several seconds before retracting the tongue back into the mouth. Next, stretch the tongue upwards towards the roof of the mouth, striving to touch the roof with the tip of the tongue. Hold this position briefly before relaxing the tongue back to its resting position. Finally, stretch the tongue downwards towards the floor of the mouth, aiming to reach as far down as possible without straining. Repeat these stretches several times, gradually increasing the duration and intensity of the stretches as your tongue flexibility improves.

Tongue push-ups, on the other hand, focus on strengthening the tongue muscles and improving coordination. To perform tongue push-ups, start by pressing the tip of your tongue firmly against the roof of your mouth, just behind the front teeth. Apply gentle pressure to the roof of the mouth with the tongue, holding the position for a few seconds before releasing. Repeat this process several times, gradually increasing the duration and intensity of the tongue presses. As you become more proficient, experiment with different tongue positions, such as pressing the sides or back of the tongue against the roof of the mouth, to target different muscle groups and enhance overall tongue strength and coordination.

By incorporating these exercises into their daily practice routine, learners can gradually improve their tongue agility and flexibility, leading to clearer and more precise pronunciation. With consistent practice and dedication, learners can develop the control and coordination necessary to produce sounds accurately and articulate words with clarity and confidence.

Furthermore, tongue placement exercises can be tailored to address individual pronunciation issues and preferences. Learners can work with a language tutor or speech coach to identify specific areas for improvement and develop customized exercises to target those areas. By incorporating these exercises into their daily practice routine, learners can make steady progress toward mastering pronunciation and achieving greater clarity and precision in their speech.

In summary, mastering pronunciation requires dedicated practice and attention to detail. Tongue placement exercises offer a valuable tool for strengthening pronunciation skills and overcoming common challenges in speech. By focusing on specific techniques and exercises, learners can develop greater control and coordination in articulating sounds, leading to clearer and more accurate pronunciation. With consistent practice and guidance, learners can improve their pronunciation skills and communicate with confidence and clarity in any language or dialect.

Action Task: Incorporate tongue placement exercises into your daily pronunciation practice routine. Focus on mastering sounds that are challenging for you, such as tongue twisters or phonetic drills targeting specific consonant or vowel sounds. Pay close attention to the position of your tongue and mouth as you articulate each sound, aiming for clarity and precision in your pronunciation. Consistent practice is key to mastering difficult sounds and improving overall pronunciation proficiency.

In addition to tongue placement exercises, consider practicing pronunciation drills that target common pronunciation challenges in your target language or dialect. For example, if you struggle with the pronunciation of certain consonant clusters or vowel sounds, dedicate focused practice sessions to these areas, gradually increasing the level of difficulty as you become more comfortable.

3.3 Seeking Feedback on Pronunciation

Feedback serves as a critical tool in the journey of refining our pronunciation skills and ensuring accuracy and clarity in our speech. Seeking feedback from trusted sources provides valuable insights and guidance that allow us to identify areas for improvement and address any pronunciation issues that may hinder effective communication. Whether from language instructors, speech coaches, peers, or native speakers, feedback offers constructive observations and suggestions for enhancing pronunciation proficiency.

One of the primary benefits of feedback is its ability to provide an external perspective on our pronunciation. While we may have our own perceptions of how we sound when speaking, feedback from others offers an objective evaluation of our pronunciation accuracy and clarity. Trusted sources can offer insights into aspects such as articulation, intonation, rhythm, and stress patterns, highlighting areas where improvement is needed and offering strategies for refinement.

Additionally, feedback allows us to identify pronunciation errors or habits that we may be unaware of. Certain pronunciation issues, such as mispronounced sounds or incorrect stress patterns, can become ingrained over time without us realizing it. Feedback from knowledgeable sources can help bring these issues to our attention, allowing us to address them proactively and work towards more accurate and clear pronunciation.

Moreover, feedback provides guidance and direction for targeted practice and improvement. By receiving specific observations and suggestions from trusted sources, we gain clarity on which aspects of our pronunciation require attention and how to approach practicing them effectively. Whether through targeted exercises, drills, or focused practice sessions, feedback informs our practice regimen and guides us towards meaningful progress.

Action Task: Record yourself speaking in your target language or dialect and listen to the recording with a critical ear. Pay attention to your pronunciation, noting any areas where clarity or accuracy could be improved. Are there specific sounds or words that you struggle to pronounce correctly? Are there patterns of pronunciation errors that recur frequently?

Once you have identified areas for improvement, seek feedback from a trusted friend, language partner, or language coach. Share your recording with them and ask for their honest assessment of your pronunciation. Request specific feedback on areas that you have identified as challenging, and be open to constructive criticism and suggestions for improvement.

Use the feedback provided by your trusted source to refine your pronunciation skills and address any pronunciation issues identified. Practice incorporating their suggestions into your pronunciation practice routine, focusing on areas that require additional attention and reinforcement. Regular feedback and self-assessment are essential for ongoing improvement in pronunciation proficiency.

In summary, feedback plays a crucial role in refining our pronunciation skills and ensuring accuracy and clarity in our speech. Seeking feedback from trusted sources allows us to gain valuable insights, identify areas for improvement, and receive guidance and direction for targeted practice and improvement. By incorporating feedback into our pronunciation practice regimen, we can refine our skills, address pronunciation issues, and communicate with greater clarity and confidence.

Action Task: Record yourself speaking in your target language or dialect and listen to the recording with a critical ear. Pay attention to your pronunciation, noting any areas where clarity or accuracy could be improved. Are there specific sounds or words that you struggle to pronounce correctly? Are there patterns of pronunciation errors that recur frequently?

Chapter 4:
Breathing and Vocal Exercises

In the realm of effective communication, mastering the art of breathing and vocal exercises holds paramount importance. These exercises are not only instrumental in nurturing a resonant and clear voice but also in enhancing the expressiveness and dynamism of speech. In this chapter, we delve into the significance of breath control in speech, explore vocal warm-up routines to prepare the voice for speaking, and discuss techniques for incorporating vocal dynamics to add interest and expressiveness to speech.

4.1 The Importance of Breath Control in Speech

Breath control serves as the cornerstone of effective communication, providing the foundation upon which clear, resonant, and authoritative speech is built. It plays a pivotal role in supporting vocal production, maintaining steady airflow, and projecting the voice with clarity and authority. By mastering breath control, speakers can enhance their vocal clarity, endurance, and overall effectiveness in conveying their message.

At its core, breath control involves the regulation and coordination of airflow during speech production. Proper breath control ensures that an adequate supply of air is available to power the vocal folds, allowing for sustained phonation and projection of sound. This steady airflow provides the necessary support for vocal production, enabling speakers to articulate words with clarity and precision.

One of the key benefits of mastering breath control is the ability to project the voice with clarity and authority. When speakers have control over their breath, they can modulate the intensity and volume of their voice to suit the demands of the speaking situation. Whether addressing a large audience or engaging in one-on-one conversation, speakers with effective breath control can project their voice with confidence and impact, commanding attention and conveying their message with authority.

Experimenting with different breathing techniques can significantly enhance breath support for speaking. One commonly practiced technique is belly breathing, also known as diaphragmatic breathing. Belly breathing involves engaging the diaphragm to draw air deep into the lungs, allowing for maximum breath support and control. By focusing on expanding the abdomen rather than the chest during inhalation, speakers can ensure a consistent and steady flow of air for vocalization.

In addition to belly breathing, other techniques such as paced breathing and breath support exercises can also help improve breath control for speaking. Paced breathing involves regulating the timing and duration of inhalation and exhalation to ensure a steady and consistent airflow. Breath support exercises focus on strengthening the muscles involved in breath control, such as the diaphragm and intercostal muscles, through targeted exercises and drills.

By incorporating these breathing techniques into your daily practice routine, you can develop greater control over your breath and enhance the clarity, resonance, and endurance of your voice. Consistent practice and experimentation with different techniques are key to mastering breath control and harnessing its power to optimize your vocal performance.

In summary, breath control lies at the core of effective communication, serving as the foundation upon which clear, resonant, and authoritative speech is built. By mastering breath control through experimentation with different breathing techniques, speakers can enhance their vocal clarity, endurance, and overall effectiveness in conveying their message. With practice and dedication, speakers can unlock the full potential of their voice and communicate with confidence and impact in any speaking situation.

4.2 Vocal Warm-Up Routines

Just like athletes warm up their muscles before physical exertion, speakers need to warm up their voices before engaging in extended periods of speaking. Vocal warm-up routines are indispensable for readying the voice for speaking engagements, as they help loosen tension in the vocal muscles, promote optimal vocal production, and prevent vocal strain. Incorporating a personalized vocal warm-up routine into your pre-speaking regimen is crucial for enhancing vocal flexibility, improving overall vocal quality, and ensuring a confident and effective delivery.

The human voice is a complex instrument, consisting of various muscles, tissues, and structures that work together to produce sound. Just as a musical instrument needs tuning and warming up before a performance, so too does the voice require preparation to function at its best. Without adequate warm-up, the vocal folds may be stiff and tense, leading to strained and fatigued vocal production, and increasing the risk of vocal injury.

Vocal warm-up routines serve several purposes in preparing the voice for speaking. Firstly, they help to loosen tension in the vocal muscles, allowing for greater flexibility and range of motion. Tense muscles can impede the free vibration of the vocal folds, resulting in a strained or constricted voice quality. By engaging in vocal warm-up exercises, speakers can release tension in the neck, throat, and jaw, promoting a more relaxed and resonant vocal production.

Secondly, vocal warm-up routines promote optimal vocal production by stimulating blood flow to the vocal folds and surrounding tissues. Increased blood flow delivers oxygen and nutrients to the vocal folds, enhancing their elasticity and resilience. This, in turn, improves vocal endurance and reduces the risk of vocal fatigue during prolonged speaking engagements.

Action Task: Begin by incorporating a series of gentle vocal warm-up exercises into your pre-speaking routine. Start by performing simple lip trills or humming exercises to gently engage the vocal folds and warm up the vocal muscles. Gradually increase the intensity of the exercises, incorporating scales, sirens, and vocal exercises targeting different areas of the vocal range. Pay attention to any areas of tension or discomfort and adjust your warm-up routine accordingly.

In addition to physical warm-up exercises, it is also important to engage in vocalization exercises that focus on articulation, resonance, and projection. These exercises help to refine vocal clarity and precision, ensuring that your message is conveyed clearly and effectively to your audience.

Lastly, vocal warm-up routines help to prepare the voice for the specific demands of the speaking engagement. Whether delivering a presentation, participating in a meeting, or engaging in public speaking, each speaking situation presents unique challenges and requirements for vocal production. By tailoring your warm-up routine to the specific demands of the speaking engagement, you can ensure that your voice is primed and ready to meet the challenges ahead.

By incorporating a personalized vocal warm-up routine into your pre-speaking regimen, you can prevent vocal strain, improve vocal flexibility, and enhance overall vocal quality. Consistent practice of vocal warm-up exercises will not only prepare your voice for the rigors of speaking but also instill confidence and assurance in your delivery. So, take the time to warm up your voice before every speaking engagement, and reap the benefits of a strong, resilient, and confident voice.

4.3 Incorporating Vocal Dynamics

In addition to mastering breath control and vocal warm-up exercises, integrating vocal dynamics into your speech can significantly enhance the impact and effectiveness of your delivery. Vocal dynamics encompass variations in tone, pitch, volume, and pace, which allow speakers to convey emotion, emphasis, and nuance in their communication. By practicing vocal dynamics in a controlled environment, speakers can develop greater versatility and expressiveness in their speech, ultimately enhancing their ability to engage and captivate their audience.

Imagine a speaker delivering a monotonous presentation with a flat tone and consistent volume throughout. While the content may be informative, the lack of vocal variation can make it dull and uninspiring for the audience. Now, picture another speaker who uses vocal dynamics to convey excitement, urgency, and conviction. By varying their tone, pitch, volume, and pace, this speaker captures the audience's attention and keeps them engaged from start to finish.

Vocal dynamics allow speakers to infuse their delivery with emotion and energy, making their message more compelling and memorable. By modulating their tone, speakers can convey warmth, enthusiasm, or authority, depending on the context of their speech. Similarly, adjusting pitch can add musicality and rhythm to the speech, creating a dynamic and engaging delivery.

Action Task: Practice varying your vocal dynamics in a controlled environment, such as during rehearsals or informal conversations. Experiment with different tones, pitches, volumes, and paces to convey a range of emotions and attitudes. Start by recording yourself speaking and listen back to identify areas where you can incorporate more vocal variation. Notice how subtle changes in tone, pitch, volume, and pace can significantly impact the effectiveness of your delivery.

Incorporating vocal dynamics into your speech requires a combination of practice, experimentation, and self-awareness. It's essential to be mindful of your natural speaking tendencies and consciously work on expanding your vocal repertoire. By regularly practicing vocal dynamics exercises, you can develop greater versatility and expressiveness in your speech, enhancing your ability to connect with and captivate your audience.

Moreover, mastering vocal dynamics can help speakers convey emphasis and nuance in their communication. By adjusting volume and pace, speakers can draw attention to key points or ideas, highlighting their importance and ensuring they resonate with the audience. Similarly, variations in tone and pitch can convey subtle shades of meaning, adding depth and richness to the speaker's message.

Incorporating vocal dynamics into your speech is essential for engaging and captivating your audience. By mastering variations in tone, pitch, volume, and pace, speakers can convey emotion, emphasis, and nuance in their communication, making their message more compelling and memorable. With practice and dedication, speakers can develop greater versatility and expressiveness in their speech, ultimately enhancing their ability to connect with and inspire their audience.

Mastering breath control and vocal exercises is essential for enhancing clarity, resonance, and expressiveness in speech. By experimenting with different breathing techniques, developing personalized vocal warm-up routines, and incorporating vocal dynamics into your delivery, you can optimize your vocal performance and captivate your audience with clear, resonant, and engaging speech. Consistent practice and attention to detail are key to mastering these techniques and unlocking your full potential as a communicator.

Chapter 5:
Pace and Pauses

In the realm of effective communication, the art of pacing and strategic pauses holds immense significance. The pace at which we speak and the strategic use of pauses can greatly impact the clarity, emphasis, and overall effectiveness of our communication. In this chapter, we will explore the importance of recognizing the impact of pace and pauses, adjusting pace for effective communication, and harnessing the power of strategic pauses to enhance our delivery.

5.1 Recognizing the Impact of Pace and Pauses

Pace and pauses are fundamental components of effective communication, exerting a significant influence on how our message is delivered and understood. The pace at which we speak directly impacts listener engagement, comprehension, and retention of information. Similarly, strategic pauses serve to emphasize key points, provide moments for reflection, and guide the listener's attention to critical aspects of our message. By analyzing recordings of speeches or presentations, we can glean valuable insights into how speakers leverage pace and pauses to enhance clarity, emphasis, and overall effectiveness in their communication.

The Pace of Speech:
The pace at which we speak is essentially the speed or rate of our delivery. It's like the tempo of a piece of music—it sets the rhythm and tone of our communication. A fast-paced delivery can be invigorating and captivating for an audience, infusing the message with energy and conveying a sense of excitement or urgency. Picture a motivational speaker rallying a crowd or a dynamic storyteller holding listeners spellbound with their rapid-fire narrative.

However, there's a delicate balance to strike. Speaking too quickly can have its drawbacks. It's like trying to drink from a firehose—there's just too much coming at you at once. For listeners, a rapid-fire delivery can feel overwhelming, leaving them struggling to keep up and process the flood of information. In such cases, even the most compelling message can get lost in the shuffle, diminishing its impact and effectiveness.

Conversely, speaking too slowly can lead to a different set of challenges. Like watching paint dry, a leisurely pace can bore or disengage listeners, causing them to tune out or lose interest in the message. It's like waiting for a snail to cross the finish line—it tests patience and can leave audiences yearning for something more stimulating. In these instances, even the most captivating content can fall flat if delivered at a sluggish pace.

Finding the right balance is key. It's about maintaining a pace that keeps listeners engaged and allows them to comfortably absorb and process the information being conveyed. Like navigating a winding road, it requires a keen sense of awareness and adaptability. By striking the right tempo, speakers can ensure that their message resonates with their audience, leaving a lasting impression long after the words have been spoken.

Action Task: To understand the impact of pace on communication, analyze recordings of speeches or presentations delivered at varying speeds. Notice how a fast-paced delivery can create a sense of momentum and energy, driving the narrative forward and maintaining listener engagement. Conversely, observe how a slower pace allows for greater clarity and comprehension, giving listeners time to absorb and process information. Reflect on the balance between pace and comprehension, and consider how you can adjust your own speaking pace to optimize listener engagement and understanding.

Strategic Pauses:
Strategic pauses are like punctuation marks in spoken language—deliberate breaks or intervals strategically inserted into speech for a variety of purposes. They serve as moments of punctuation, allowing speakers to emphasize key points, facilitate reflection, or signal transitions between ideas. Just as a well-placed comma or period can enhance the clarity and flow of written text, strategic pauses play a similar role in spoken communication.

Pauses come in various lengths and timings, ranging from brief hesitations to extended silences, depending on the desired effect and the context of the communication. A brief pause can draw attention to a significant point, allowing it to resonate with the audience and reinforcing its importance. Meanwhile, an extended pause can create suspense or anticipation, holding the listener's attention and heightening the impact of the message.

When used effectively, strategic pauses can significantly enhance the clarity, emphasis, and overall effectiveness of communication. They provide valuable moments for listeners to digest and internalize information, making it easier for them to follow the speaker's train of thought and retain key points. Additionally, pauses can help break up dense or complex information, allowing listeners to process it more easily and preventing cognitive overload.

Action Task: To understand the power of strategic pauses, analyze recordings of speeches or presentations where speakers employ pauses to great effect. Notice how a well-placed pause can add emphasis and gravitas to a key point, allowing it to stand out and resonate with the audience. Pay attention to the timing and duration of the pauses, and how they contribute to the overall rhythm and flow of the speech. Consider how you can incorporate similar techniques into your own communication style to enhance clarity, emphasis, and overall effectiveness.

Strategic pauses are a powerful tool in the speaker's arsenal, allowing for greater clarity, emphasis, and engagement in communication. By mastering the art of strategic pausing, speakers can create more compelling and impactful presentations, effectively guiding their audience through the journey of their message and leaving a lasting impression.

By analyzing recordings of speeches or presentations, we can gain valuable insights into the art of pacing and strategic pauses in communication. Whether speaking quickly to build excitement or pausing strategically to emphasize key points, speakers can leverage pace and pauses to enhance clarity, emphasis, and overall effectiveness in delivering their message. With practice and awareness, we can refine our own communication skills and become more adept at leveraging pace and pauses to engage and captivate our audience..

Action Task: To recognize the impact of pace and pauses, analyze recordings of speeches or presentations, paying close attention to how speakers vary their pace and incorporate pauses for emphasis and clarity. Notice how changes in pace can create tension, build suspense, or convey urgency, while well-timed pauses can allow for reflection, emphasize important points, or signal transitions between ideas. Take note of the effects of pace and pauses on listener engagement and comprehension, and consider how you can apply these techniques to your own communication style.

By developing awareness of the impact of pace and pauses, we can better understand how to utilize these elements effectively to enhance our delivery and engage our audience.

5.2 Adjusting Pace for Effective Communication

The pace at which we speak holds immense sway over listener comprehension and engagement. It's akin to finding the right tempo in a musical composition—a balance that can make all the difference in how our message is received. When we speak too quickly, it's like trying to pour water from a firehose—there's just too much coming at the listener too fast. This can lead to a sense of overwhelm and confusion, making it difficult for them to keep up and grasp the content being conveyed. Conversely, speaking too slowly can have a different but equally detrimental effect. It's like watching paint dry—a slow, laborious process that can lull the audience into disinterest or boredom.

Finding the sweet spot in our speaking pace is crucial. It's about gauging the needs of our audience and the context of the communication and adjusting accordingly. When delivering complex or dense information, slowing down can provide clarity and ensure that listeners have the opportunity to absorb and process each point. On the other hand, when trying to build excitement or momentum, picking up the pace can inject energy and captivate the audience's attention.

Action Task: Reflect on recent speaking experiences and consider how your pace impacted audience comprehension and engagement. Were there instances where you noticed listeners struggling to keep up or appearing disengaged? Conversely, were there moments where you felt you lost their interest due to speaking too slowly? Take note of these observations and use them to inform your future speaking engagements. Practice adjusting your pace to suit the needs of the audience and the context, aiming for a rhythm that fosters comprehension and engagement.

In essence, adjusting our speaking pace is an essential skill in effective communication. By finding the right tempo, we can ensure that our message is delivered with clarity and impact, resonating with our audience and leaving a lasting impression. So, whether racing ahead or taking it slow, let's strive to strike the perfect balance in our speaking pace, captivating our audience and conveying our message with precision and power.

Action Task: To adjust pace for effective communication, experiment with slowing down your speech in situations where clarity is paramount. Practice enunciating each word clearly and maintaining a steady pace to enhance listener comprehension. Pay attention to your natural speaking rhythm and make conscious efforts to slow down when necessary, especially when introducing new concepts, explaining complex ideas, or delivering important information. Notice how slowing down your pace can improve listener comprehension and retention of information, and incorporate this technique into your communication repertoire.

In addition to slowing down your pace, it's also important to vary your pace to maintain listener engagement and interest. By incorporating changes in pace, such as speeding up during exciting or suspenseful moments and slowing down during reflective or profound moments, you can create a dynamic and engaging delivery that captures the audience's attention and keeps them invested in your message.

By adjusting your pace to suit the needs of the audience and the context of the communication, you can enhance listener comprehension, engagement, and retention of information, ultimately leading to more effective communication outcomes.

5.3 Harnessing the Power of Strategic Pauses

Strategic pauses are like punctuation marks in the symphony of speech—they provide moments of silence strategically inserted into our communication to serve various purposes. Much like a conductor directing a musical performance, we can use these pauses to orchestrate the rhythm, emphasis, and flow of our delivery, enhancing the impact and effectiveness of our message.

Pauses offer a wealth of opportunities for enhancing communication. They allow for reflection, giving listeners the space to digest and internalize information before moving on to the next point. By punctuating our speech with deliberate pauses, we can emphasize important points, giving them the weight and attention they deserve. These strategic pauses guide the listener's attention, directing them to key ideas and ensuring that they remain engaged and focused throughout the discourse.

Action Task: To harness the power of strategic pauses, begin by practicing their incorporation into your speech. Start by identifying key points or moments in your message where a pause could serve to enhance clarity or emphasis. Pause briefly after introducing new ideas or concepts, allowing listeners a moment to process the information before continuing. For particularly impactful points, consider using longer pauses to draw attention and emphasize their significance. Experiment with varying the length and timing of pauses to create rhythm and maintain listener engagement, paying attention to how each pause affects the overall flow and clarity of your delivery.

Let's consider a speech about the importance of environmental conservation. Here's an excerpt from the speech with suggested places where strategic pauses could be incorporated:

"Good evening, ladies and gentlemen. Today, I stand before you to address a matter of utmost urgency—the preservation of our planet's precious natural resources. It's no secret that our world is facing an unprecedented environmental crisis, one that threatens the very existence of life as we know it.

Pause: [Brief pause for emphasis and to allow listeners to mentally prepare for the gravity of the topic.]

"As we go about our daily lives, it's easy to overlook the impact of our actions on the environment. We consume resources at an alarming rate, heedless of the consequences for future generations. But make no mistake—every plastic bottle tossed into the ocean, every tree felled in the name of progress—these are not just isolated incidents. They are part of a larger pattern of destruction that is pushing our planet to the brink of collapse.

Pause: [Longer pause to allow listeners to absorb the seriousness of the situation and reflect on their own behaviors.]

"But it's not too late to change course. We have the power to make a difference, to be stewards of the earth and protectors of its biodiversity. Through small, everyday actions—like reducing our carbon footprint, conserving water, and supporting sustainable practices—we can mitigate the damage and pave the way for a greener, more sustainable future.

Pause: [Brief pause to underscore the importance of individual action and allow listeners to consider how they can contribute.]

"Together, we can forge a path towards environmental sustainability—a path marked by conservation, innovation, and collective responsibility. Let us rise to the challenge before us, not as passive bystanders, but as active participants in the fight to preserve our planet for generations to come.

Pause: [Final pause for emphasis and to allow the message to resonate with the audience before concluding the speech.]"

In this example, strategic pauses are used to emphasize key points, allow for reflection, and guide the audience's attention. By incorporating pauses thoughtfully into the delivery, the speaker enhances the clarity, emphasis, and overall effectiveness of the message, ensuring that it leaves a lasting impression on the audience.

Action Point:
Take a moment to practice delivering the speech on environmental conservation with the suggested pauses. Stand in front of a mirror or record yourself speaking to simulate the experience of addressing an audience. As you deliver each segment of the speech, consciously incorporate the strategic pauses at the indicated points:

1. Begin by delivering the opening lines of the speech, pausing briefly after the introductory remarks to allow listeners to mentally prepare for the gravity of the topic.

2. Continue with the main body of the speech, incorporating longer pauses after discussing the severity of the environmental crisis to allow listeners to absorb the seriousness of the situation and reflect on their own behaviors.

3. After highlighting the potential for positive change through individual actions, insert a brief pause to underscore the importance of personal responsibility and give listeners a moment to consider how they can contribute.

4. Conclude the speech with a final pause for emphasis, allowing the message to resonate with the audience before wrapping up.

Repeat this practice several times, focusing on maintaining a steady pace and incorporating the pauses naturally into your delivery. Pay attention to how the strategic pauses enhance the clarity, emphasis, and overall effectiveness of your speech, and make adjustments as needed to refine your delivery. With consistent practice, you'll build confidence in using pauses as a powerful tool for engaging and resonating with your audience.

As you integrate strategic pauses into your communication style, you'll notice their transformative effects. Not only do they enhance clarity and emphasis, but they also create anticipation and suspense, keeping the audience engaged and eager to hear what comes next. Like the pregnant pause before a punchline in a joke, these moments of silence heighten the impact of our words, leaving a lasting impression on our listeners.

Mastering the art of strategic pauses is a powerful tool for enhancing the impact and effectiveness of our communication. By incorporating pauses thoughtfully and intentionally into our speech, we can create rhythm, build suspense, and elevate the overall clarity and flow of our delivery. So, embrace the power of the pause, and let its silent eloquence speak volumes in your communication.

In summary, pace and pauses are essential elements of effective communication, influencing listener engagement, comprehension, and retention of information. By recognizing the impact of pace and pauses, adjusting our pace for effective communication, and harnessing the power of strategic pauses, we can enhance the clarity, emphasis, and overall effectiveness of our delivery, ultimately leading to more engaging and impactful communication outcomes.

Chapter 6:
Listening Skills

Listening is an essential component of effective communication, yet it is often overlooked or undervalued. In this chapter, we will explore the importance of developing strong listening skills and provide actionable strategies for improving your ability to listen actively, comprehend information, and provide constructive feedback.

6.1 Developing Active Listening Habits

Active listening is not merely a passive act of hearing words; it is a dynamic process that involves fully engaging with the speaker and demonstrating genuine attentiveness and empathy. It goes beyond simply registering the sounds and meanings of words; it requires understanding the underlying message, both verbal and nonverbal, and responding in a manner that acknowledges and validates the speaker's perspective. Developing active listening habits is crucial for building strong interpersonal connections, fostering trust, and enhancing communication effectiveness in various contexts.

At its essence, active listening embodies the art of being wholly present in the moment, offering the speaker your complete and undivided attention. It demands a deliberate choice to set aside distractions, whether they be external, like buzzing smartphones or ambient noise, or internal, such as wandering thoughts or preoccupations. Instead, the focus is singular: on the speaker and the message they are conveying.

By committing to active listening, you not only honor the speaker but also validate their experience. This act of genuine interest and attentiveness communicates a profound sense of respect, fostering an environment where open and honest communication can flourish. When the speaker feels heard and valued, they are more likely to express themselves authentically, leading to richer and more meaningful interactions.

Imagine a scenario where a friend is sharing their struggles with you. Active listening requires you to set aside any distractions, like checking your phone or thinking about your own problems, and instead, focus entirely on your friend's words and emotions. You maintain eye contact, nodding occasionally to signal your understanding and encouragement. You refrain from interrupting or offering solutions prematurely, allowing your friend the space to express themselves fully.

In doing so, you create a safe and supportive space where your friend feels heard and understood. Your genuine interest and attentiveness convey respect and validation, affirming the importance of their experiences. This, in turn, encourages them to share more openly and honestly, deepening the trust and connection between you.

Active listening is not merely a passive act; it is a conscious choice to engage fully with another person, to empathize with their experiences, and to validate their feelings. It requires discipline and intentionality but yields immense rewards in terms of building relationships, fostering trust, and promoting effective communication. By making active listening a cornerstone of your interactions, you can create meaningful connections and cultivate a culture of respect and understanding in your personal and professional relationships.

Empathy is another aspect of active listening, as it involves not only hearing the speaker's words but also understanding their emotions, perspectives, and underlying needs. When we practice empathetic listening, we make a conscious effort to put ourselves in the speaker's shoes, seeing the world from their perspective and seeking to comprehend their thoughts and feelings.

Empathetic listening requires us to tune into both verbal and nonverbal cues, recognizing that communication extends beyond words alone. We pay attention to the speaker's tone of voice, volume, and inflection, as well as their choice of words and language patterns. Additionally, we observe their facial expressions, gestures, and body language, which often convey emotions and intentions more powerfully than words.

For example, imagine a colleague sharing their concerns about a challenging project. As an empathetic listener, you not only listen to their words but also tune into their tone of voice, noting any signs of frustration, anxiety, or excitement. You observe their body language, noticing if they appear tense, relaxed, or animated. By paying attention to these cues, you gain insight into their emotional state and can respond with empathy and understanding.

By demonstrating empathy, you show the speaker that you care about their experiences and are invested in their well-being. This acknowledgment of their emotions and perspectives fosters a sense of validation and acceptance, creating a safe space for them to express themselves openly and honestly. In turn, this fosters deeper trust and connection in the relationship, as the speaker feels genuinely heard and understood.

Moreover, empathy enhances the effectiveness of communication by facilitating deeper levels of understanding and connection. When we empathize with others, we are better able to grasp their motivations, concerns, and needs, allowing us to respond with greater sensitivity and insight. This promotes smoother and more meaningful interactions, where mutual respect and understanding form the foundation for constructive dialogue and collaboration.

Empathy is a vital component of active listening, enabling us to understand and connect with others on a deeper level. By tuning into verbal and nonverbal cues, demonstrating empathy, and acknowledging the speaker's emotions and perspectives, we foster trust, build rapport, and promote effective communication in all aspects of our lives..

Developing active listening habits is essential for building rapport and strengthening relationships in both personal and professional settings. When people feel heard and understood, they are more likely to open up and share their thoughts and feelings openly. This, in turn, can lead to more meaningful and productive interactions, where ideas are exchanged freely, and conflicts are resolved amicably.

In addition to building rapport and fostering trust, active listening enhances communication effectiveness by ensuring mutual understanding and clarity. By actively engaging with the speaker and seeking to comprehend their message fully, you can avoid misunderstandings and misinterpretations that often arise from passive listening or distracted communication. This promotes smoother and more efficient communication, where ideas are conveyed accurately and objectives are achieved effectively.

Active listening is a fundamental skill that is essential for effective communication. By fully engaging with the speaker, demonstrating attentiveness and empathy, and seeking to understand the underlying message, you can build rapport, foster trust, and enhance communication effectiveness in various contexts. By cultivating active listening habits, you can become a more attentive and empathetic communicator, creating meaningful connections and achieving better outcomes in your interactions with others.

Action Task: Practice active listening techniques in your daily interactions. During conversations, make a conscious effort to maintain eye contact with the speaker, nodding occasionally to signal understanding and encouragement. Summarize key points or ask clarifying questions to demonstrate your engagement and ensure mutual understanding. Avoid distractions and resist the urge to interrupt or formulate responses prematurely. By actively listening to others, you can cultivate stronger interpersonal relationships and improve communication outcomes.

6.2 Improving Listening Comprehension

Listening comprehension is a multifaceted skill that goes beyond simply hearing the words spoken by others. It encompasses the ability to understand and interpret spoken language accurately, processing not only the literal meaning of the words but also their underlying context, nuances, and implications. Strengthening your listening comprehension skills is essential for effectively extracting valuable information from various sources and engaging in meaningful dialogue with others.

At its core, listening comprehension involves actively engaging with spoken language, whether it be in conversations, lectures, podcasts, or presentations. It requires not only hearing the words being spoken but also decoding their meaning, synthesizing information, and making connections between ideas. This process involves drawing upon your existing knowledge and experiences to interpret the message accurately and derive deeper insights.

Listening comprehension is about more than just understanding individual words or phrases; it involves grasping the broader context and purpose behind the communication. This includes considering factors such as tone of voice, emphasis, and pacing, as well as nonverbal cues like facial expressions and body language, which can convey additional layers of meaning.

Strengthening your listening comprehension skills requires practice and deliberate effort. One effective strategy is to actively engage with a variety of spoken content, such as podcasts, audiobooks, lectures, or TED talks, on topics that interest you. By exposing yourself to diverse sources of spoken language, you can expand your vocabulary, improve your understanding of different accents and dialects, and develop greater fluency in comprehension.

As you listen to spoken content, it can be helpful to take notes or jot down key points to reinforce your understanding and retention of the material. Summarizing what you've heard in your own words can also be an effective way to solidify your comprehension and identify any areas of confusion or uncertainty.

In addition to consuming spoken content, engaging in active listening practices in everyday conversations can also help improve your listening comprehension skills. This involves giving the speaker your full attention, asking clarifying questions when necessary, and paraphrasing what you've heard to ensure mutual understanding. By practicing active listening in your interactions with others, you can enhance your ability to comprehend spoken language and engage more effectively in dialogue.

In summary, listening comprehension is a critical skill that underpins effective communication and meaningful engagement with others. By actively engaging with spoken content, practicing active listening techniques, and seeking to understand the broader context and purpose behind communication, you can strengthen your listening comprehension skills and become a more effective communicator in all areas of your life.

Action Task: Challenge yourself to expand your listening repertoire by exploring podcasts, audiobooks, or lectures on topics outside your comfort zone. Select content that interests you but also introduces new ideas or perspectives. As you listen, take notes to capture key concepts and insights. Summarize what you've heard in your own words to reinforce understanding and retention. Gradually increase the complexity of the material you engage with to push your listening comprehension skills to new heights.

6.3 Providing Constructive Feedback

Effective communication is indeed a dynamic process that requires active participation from both parties involved. It is not just about transmitting information but also about receiving feedback and engaging in meaningful dialogue. In this regard, communication can be likened to a two-way street where both listening and providing feedback play integral roles in fostering understanding and driving growth.

Providing feedback is a critical aspect of effective communication, as it offers valuable insights and perspectives that contribute to personal and professional development. Constructive feedback, in particular, serves as a catalyst for promoting growth and improvement in speaking skills and creating a supportive learning environment where individuals can thrive.

Constructive feedback is a cornerstone of personal and professional growth, particularly in the realm of speaking skills. Unlike criticism or judgment, which can be demoralizing and unproductive, constructive feedback is characterized by its focus on specific behaviors or actions, rather than personal attributes. It aims to provide actionable insights and suggestions for improvement, empowering individuals to enhance their skills and reach their full potential.

In the context of speaking skills, constructive feedback addresses various aspects of communication, such as clarity, articulation, pacing, and vocal tone. For example, a speaker may receive feedback on their delivery style, with suggestions for improving vocal projection or incorporating more varied intonation to captivate the audience's attention. Similarly, feedback on language usage, including grammar, vocabulary, or word choice, can help speakers refine their communication skills and express themselves more effectively.

By highlighting areas of strength and offering guidance for development, constructive feedback creates a supportive environment where individuals feel empowered to grow and improve. Rather than feeling discouraged by criticism, they are motivated to take action and implement positive changes in their communication approach. Moreover, constructive feedback fosters a culture of continuous learning and development, where individuals are encouraged to seek out opportunities for improvement and strive for excellence in their speaking skills.

Constructive feedback serves as a catalyst for personal and professional growth, enabling individuals to refine their communication abilities and achieve greater success in their endeavors. By providing specific and actionable feedback in a supportive and respectful manner, we can empower others to unlock their full potential and excel in their speaking skills.

Furthermore, constructive feedback plays a crucial role in fostering a supportive learning environment where individuals feel safe to take risks and make mistakes. By providing constructive feedback in a respectful and nonjudgmental manner, we create opportunities for growth and encourage continuous learning. When individuals feel supported and encouraged to improve, they are more likely to take ownership of their development and strive for excellence in their communication skills.

In summary, effective communication is indeed a two-way street that involves both listening and providing feedback. Constructive feedback is essential for promoting growth and improvement in speaking skills, as well as fostering a supportive learning environment where individuals feel empowered to develop their communication abilities. By offering specific and actionable feedback in a respectful and supportive manner, we can empower others to reach their full potential and excel in their communication endeavors.

Action Task: Practice giving constructive feedback to peers, colleagues, or family members on their speaking skills. Focus on specific areas for improvement, such as articulation, pacing, or vocal tone. Offer supportive suggestions for growth, highlighting strengths and providing actionable recommendations for development. Remember to deliver feedback in a respectful and constructive manner, focusing on behaviors rather than personal attributes. By offering thoughtful and encouraging feedback, you can help others enhance their communication skills and achieve their full potential.

In conclusion, developing strong listening skills is essential for effective communication. By actively engaging with others, improving listening comprehension, and providing constructive feedback, you can become a more attentive and empathetic communicator, fostering meaningful connections and achieving better communication outcomes in both personal and professional settings.

Chapter 7:
Overcoming Fear of Public Speaking

Public speaking anxiety, commonly known as glossophobia, is a pervasive fear that affects many individuals, regardless of their background or experience. For some, the mere thought of speaking in front of a crowd can evoke intense feelings of fear, nervousness, and self-doubt. However, with the right strategies and mindset, it is possible to overcome this fear and develop the confidence to speak effectively in public settings.

7.1 Understanding the Roots of Public Speaking Anxiety

Public speaking anxiety can be attributed to a variety of factors that intertwine to create a formidable barrier to effective communication. Among these factors are the fear of judgment, perfectionism, lack of confidence, and negative past experiences. These elements often work in concert to heighten anxiety and inhibit individuals from expressing themselves confidently in public settings.

The fear of judgment looms large as one of the primary instigators of public speaking anxiety. It's the dread of being under the microscope, scrutinized, criticized, or even ridiculed by an audience. This fear of negative evaluation strikes at the core of one's self-esteem, breeding feelings of inadequacy and self-doubt that can prove paralyzing in the face of public speaking engagements.

The thought of being subjected to judgment from others can be overwhelming, triggering a cascade of anxious thoughts and emotions. Individuals may find themselves caught in a relentless cycle of worry, imagining all the ways in which they might fall short or be found lacking in the eyes of their audience. These fears can become so consuming that individuals may go to great lengths to avoid speaking opportunities altogether, retreating into the safety of silence rather than risk facing potential judgment.

For those who do brave the stage, the fear of judgment can manifest as extreme anxiety, manifesting in physical symptoms such as trembling, sweating, or a racing heart. The fear of negative evaluation can hijack rational thought processes, leaving individuals feeling as though they are under siege, battling against an unseen enemy of their own making.

The fear of judgment is deeply rooted in the human psyche, stemming from our innate desire for acceptance and belonging. Throughout history, social rejection has been linked to survival, triggering primal instincts that warn us of potential threats to our well-being. In the context of public speaking, the fear of judgment taps into these primal fears, evoking a visceral response that can be difficult to overcome.

However, it's important to recognize that the fear of judgment is often based on irrational beliefs and perceptions. While it's natural to seek approval from others, the reality is that not everyone will respond positively to our words or ideas. Understanding that criticism is inevitable and learning to separate constructive feedback from baseless criticism is a crucial step in overcoming the fear of judgment.

Moreover, it's essential to remember that the audience is not an adversary but rather a group of individuals who are there to listen and learn. By shifting our mindset from one of fear to one of curiosity and empathy, we can transform the dynamics of public speaking from a battleground to a forum for connection and mutual understanding.

The fear of judgment can be a potent force that undermines our confidence and inhibits our ability to speak effectively in public settings. However, by acknowledging and confronting this fear head-on, we can begin to dismantle its hold over us and reclaim our power as communicators. With practice and perseverance, we can learn to speak with authenticity and conviction, free from the shackles of judgment and self-doubt.

Perfectionism casts a long shadow over public speaking, intensifying the already formidable anxiety that individuals experience in front of an audience. Those who adhere to impossibly high standards for themselves may find the prospect of speaking in public especially daunting, as they fear the consequences of falling short of perfection. This fear of failure, fueled by the relentless pursuit of flawlessness, can exact a heavy toll on one's mental and emotional well-being, leading to heightened anxiety and self-criticism.

Individuals who grapple with perfectionism often harbor deep-seated fears of making mistakes or appearing incompetent in front of others. They may feel as though any deviation from perfection will result in harsh judgment or rejection from their audience, triggering a cascade of negative thoughts and emotions. This fear of failure can be paralyzing, leaving individuals feeling overwhelmed and ill-equipped to handle the pressures of public speaking.

The pressure to deliver flawless performances can be especially burdensome for perfectionists, who may feel as though their entire self-worth is contingent upon their ability to meet impossibly high standards. Every minor mistake or imperfection is magnified in their minds, reinforcing feelings of inadequacy and self-doubt. As a result, individuals may go to great lengths to avoid speaking opportunities altogether or engage in excessive preparation in a desperate attempt to mitigate the risk of failure.

The relentless pursuit of perfection can take a significant toll on one's mental and emotional well-being, leading to heightened levels of anxiety, stress, and self-criticism. Perfectionists may engage in negative self-talk, berating themselves for any perceived shortcomings or mistakes. This constant internal dialogue of self-criticism only serves to reinforce feelings of inadequacy and erode confidence, making it even more challenging to speak confidently in public settings.

Overcoming perfectionism requires a shift in mindset and a willingness to embrace imperfection. Instead of striving for flawlessness, individuals must learn to accept themselves and their abilities as they are, recognizing that mistakes are a natural part of the learning process. By reframing failure as an opportunity for growth rather than a reflection of one's worth, individuals can cultivate greater resilience and confidence in their speaking abilities.

Moreover, it's essential to recognize that perfection is an unrealistic and unattainable standard. No one is flawless, and expecting oneself to be perfect only sets the stage for disappointment and frustration. By letting go of the need to be perfect and embracing authenticity, individuals can speak with greater confidence and conviction, free from the constraints of perfectionism.

Perfectionism exacerbates public speaking anxiety by setting impossibly high standards and fostering a fear of failure. To overcome perfectionism, individuals must learn to accept themselves and their abilities as they are, embracing imperfection as a natural part of the learning process. By letting go of the need to be perfect and embracing authenticity, individuals can speak with greater confidence and conviction, free from the constraints of perfectionism.

A lack of confidence casts a long shadow over the landscape of public speaking, serving as a significant contributor to the anxiety that many individuals experience in front of an audience. For those who struggle with low self-esteem, the prospect of speaking in public can feel like navigating a minefield of self-doubt and uncertainty. This lack of confidence can manifest in various ways, from nervousness and trembling hands to a pervasive sense of inadequacy that undermines one's ability to speak confidently and assertively.

Individuals who lack confidence often harbor deep-seated doubts about their abilities and qualifications to speak effectively in public settings. They may perceive themselves as unworthy or ill-prepared to handle the challenges of public speaking, leading to a pervasive sense of unease and self-doubt. This inner critic can be relentless, chipping away at one's self-esteem and eroding any semblance of confidence or assurance.

The lack of confidence can manifest in physical symptoms such as trembling hands, a racing heart, or a dry mouth, all of which can further exacerbate feelings of anxiety and self-doubt. These physiological responses are a natural reaction to stress, but for individuals with low self-esteem, they can feel overwhelming and debilitating, making it difficult to speak with clarity and conviction.

Moreover, the lack of confidence can create a self-perpetuating cycle of anxiety and avoidance, as individuals may shy away from speaking opportunities altogether in a bid to avoid the discomfort of feeling exposed or vulnerable. This avoidance only serves to reinforce feelings of inadequacy and erode confidence further, creating a vicious cycle that can be difficult to break.

Overcoming a lack of confidence requires a concerted effort to challenge negative self-beliefs and build self-esteem from the inside out. This process may involve identifying and reframing negative thought patterns, setting realistic goals for personal growth, and practicing self-care and self-compassion. By cultivating a positive self-image and recognizing one's inherent worth and value, individuals can begin to break free from the grip of self-doubt and speak with greater confidence and assertiveness.

Additionally, seeking support from trusted friends, mentors, or professional coaches can provide invaluable encouragement and guidance on the journey to building confidence in public speaking. By surrounding oneself with positive influences and seeking out opportunities for growth and development, individuals can gradually overcome their lack of confidence and emerge as confident and compelling communicators..

Negative past experiences wield a significant influence over public speaking anxiety, serving as potent fuel for the fears and insecurities that individuals grapple with when faced with speaking in front of an audience. Traumatic or embarrassing experiences from the past can cast a long shadow, leaving indelible scars on one's psyche and instilling a profound fear of repeating those painful episodes. As a result, individuals may develop a deep-seated aversion to public speaking, characterized by heightened anxiety and avoidance behaviors.

For those who have endured traumatic or humiliating experiences while speaking in public, the memory of those incidents can linger like a specter, haunting their thoughts and coloring their perceptions of future speaking engagements. The fear of experiencing similar humiliation or failure can be paralyzing, triggering intense anxiety and avoidance behaviors that further reinforce the cycle of fear.

These past experiences can create deep-seated psychological barriers that hinder individuals from speaking confidently and assertively in future situations. The fear of repeating past mistakes or facing judgment from others can erode one's confidence and self-esteem, making it difficult to summon the courage to speak up and share their thoughts and ideas.

Moreover, the lingering trauma from past experiences can manifest in physical symptoms such as trembling hands, a racing heart, or a dry mouth, all of which serve as painful reminders of the fear and anxiety associated with public speaking. These physiological responses are a natural reaction to stress, but for individuals who have experienced traumatic speaking experiences in the past, they can feel overwhelming and debilitating.

Overcoming the psychological barriers created by negative past experiences requires a willingness to confront and process the underlying emotions associated with those events. This may involve seeking support from a therapist or counselor who can help individuals work through their feelings of fear, shame, and inadequacy in a safe and supportive environment.

Also, gradually exposing oneself to speaking opportunities in low-pressure settings can help individuals build confidence and resilience over time. By confronting their fears head-on and gradually expanding their comfort zone, individuals can begin to dismantle the psychological barriers that have held them back and emerge as confident and capable speakers.

Ultimately, overcoming the fear associated with negative past experiences requires patience, persistence, and a commitment to self-care and self-compassion. By acknowledging the impact of past trauma and taking proactive steps to address it, individuals can reclaim their power and speak with confidence and assertiveness in future situations.

Understanding the underlying causes of public speaking anxiety is essential for addressing and managing this common fear effectively. By identifying the specific factors that contribute to their anxiety, individuals can develop targeted coping strategies to overcome their fears and build confidence in their speaking abilities. These strategies may include cognitive-behavioral techniques, relaxation exercises, exposure therapy, and positive self-talk, among others. With perseverance and practice, individuals can learn to manage their anxiety and speak confidently and assertively in public settings.

Action Task: Reflect on past experiences or beliefs that contribute to your fear of public speaking. Challenge negative perceptions and reframe them in a positive light. Consider journaling about your experiences or discussing them with a trusted friend or mentor. By gaining insight into the root causes of your anxiety, you can begin to overcome them and build greater confidence in your speaking abilities.

7.2 Building Confidence through Preparation

Thorough preparation stands as one of the most potent antidotes to public speaking anxiety, offering a robust shield against the onslaught of nerves and self-doubt that often accompany speaking in front of an audience. By investing time and effort into researching your topic, organizing your thoughts, and honing your delivery, you can cultivate a sense of confidence and competence that serves as a bulwark against anxiety in the lead-up to a speaking engagement.

Researching your topic thoroughly provides a solid foundation upon which to build your presentation. By delving deep into the subject matter, gathering relevant data, and exploring different perspectives, you can bolster your understanding and expertise, ensuring that you speak with authority and credibility. Moreover, thorough research enables you to anticipate potential questions or objections from your audience, allowing you to prepare thoughtful responses and address any concerns proactively.

Organizing your thoughts is essential for crafting a coherent and compelling message that resonates with your audience. Take the time to outline your key points, structure your presentation in a logical manner, and create a clear roadmap that guides listeners through your ideas. A well-organized presentation not only enhances comprehension but also instills a sense of confidence in both the speaker and the audience, fostering a shared understanding and connection.

Practicing your delivery is perhaps the most critical aspect of thorough preparation when it comes to combating public speaking anxiety. Repetition breeds familiarity, and by rehearsing your presentation multiple times, you can internalize your material, refine your delivery, and build confidence in your ability to communicate effectively. Practice speaking aloud in front of a mirror, recording yourself, or enlisting the help of a friend or mentor to provide feedback and support.

As you practice, pay attention to your body language, vocal tone, and pacing, making adjustments as needed to enhance clarity and engagement. Focus on maintaining steady eye contact with your audience, using gestures and facial expressions to emphasize key points, and varying your vocal inflection to keep listeners engaged. The more comfortable you become with your material and delivery, the less likely you are to succumb to anxiety when speaking in front of others.

In addition to boosting confidence, thorough preparation also helps alleviate anxiety by reducing the unknowns and uncertainties associated with speaking in public. When you know your material inside and out, you can approach your presentation with a sense of calm and assurance, knowing that you are well-equipped to handle whatever challenges may arise.

Thorough preparation is a powerful weapon in the fight against public speaking anxiety. By immersing yourself in your topic, organizing your thoughts, and practicing your delivery, you can bolster your confidence, reduce anxiety, and deliver a polished and persuasive presentation that leaves a lasting impression on your audience.

Action Task: Prepare thoroughly for speaking engagements by researching the topic, organizing your thoughts, and practicing your delivery. Start by outlining your key points and supporting evidence, and then create a clear and concise presentation structure. Practice speaking aloud in front of a mirror or recording yourself to identify areas for improvement. The more prepared you feel, the more confident you'll be when it's time to speak in front of an audience.

7.3 Gradual Exposure to Public Speaking

For countless individuals grappling with the fear of public speaking, gradual exposure and desensitization emerge as transformative strategies for overcoming anxiety and building confidence. This approach involves systematically exposing oneself to speaking opportunities in low-pressure settings, gradually acclimating to the challenges of public speaking and cultivating a sense of mastery and comfort over time.

The process of gradual exposure begins with identifying and engaging in speaking opportunities that are relatively low-stakes and manageable in terms of audience size and expectations. This might involve participating in small group discussions, delivering presentations to supportive colleagues or friends, or joining public speaking clubs or workshops where individuals can practice speaking in a safe and supportive environment.

By starting small and gradually increasing the level of exposure, individuals can incrementally expand their comfort zone and confront their fears in a controlled and manageable manner. This gradual approach allows individuals to build confidence and competence at their own pace, without feeling overwhelmed or intimidated by the prospect of speaking in front of a large audience.

As individuals gain experience and familiarity with speaking in public, they begin to develop a sense of mastery and confidence in their abilities. Each successful speaking engagement serves as a building block, reinforcing positive beliefs about one's capacity to communicate effectively and navigate the challenges of public speaking with poise and composure.

Moreover, gradual exposure provides opportunities for individuals to learn from their experiences and refine their speaking skills over time. By reflecting on each speaking opportunity and identifying areas for improvement, individuals can gain valuable insights into their strengths and weaknesses as speakers, allowing them to make targeted adjustments and enhancements to their communication style.

In addition to building confidence and competence, gradual exposure and desensitization can also help individuals reframe their perception of public speaking from a threat to an opportunity for growth and self-expression. By confronting their fears head-on and embracing the challenge of public speaking, individuals can develop resilience, grit, and a sense of empowerment that transcends the confines of the stage.

Ultimately, the journey of gradual exposure and desensitization is not about eradicating fear entirely but learning to manage and harness it in service of personal and professional growth. By embracing each speaking opportunity as a chance to learn and grow, individuals can transform their relationship with public speaking and emerge as confident, articulate, and persuasive communicators.

Action Task: Start by seeking out opportunities to speak in low-pressure settings, such as Toastmasters meetings, small group discussions, or informal presentations. Focus on building your confidence and refining your speaking skills in a supportive and nonjudgmental environment. As you become more comfortable speaking in front of others, gradually increase the size of your audience and the complexity of your presentations. With each successful speaking experience, your confidence will grow, and your fear of public speaking will diminish.

In summary, overcoming the fear of public speaking requires a combination of self-awareness, preparation, and gradual exposure. By understanding the root causes of your anxiety, preparing thoroughly for speaking engagements, and gradually exposing yourself to speaking opportunities, you can build the confidence and skills needed to speak effectively in public settings. With persistence and practice, you can overcome your fear of public speaking and become a more confident and compelling communicator.

Chapter 8:
Building Vocabulary and Language Skills

Language is a remarkable tool that allows us to communicate, connect, and express ourselves in myriad ways. At the heart of effective communication lies vocabulary—the collection of words and phrases that we use to convey our thoughts, ideas, and emotions. A rich and varied vocabulary not only enhances our ability to articulate ourselves with precision and clarity but also enriches our understanding of the world around us.

In this chapter, we will delve into the importance of building vocabulary and strengthening language skills. We'll explore strategies for expanding your lexicon, using language in context, and exploring the intricacies of language through reading. By actively engaging with these strategies, you can enhance your communication abilities, deepen your appreciation for language, and unlock new avenues for self-expression and connection.

8.1 Expanding Your Vocabulary

Language is a dynamic and ever-evolving tool of communication, serving as a vehicle for expressing thoughts, ideas, and emotions. At the core of effective communication lies vocabulary—the collection of words and phrases that we use to convey meaning and engage with others. A rich and varied vocabulary not only enhances our ability to articulate ourselves with precision and nuance but also deepens our understanding of the world around us. In this chapter, we will explore strategies for expanding your vocabulary and strengthening your language skills.

Action Task: Dedicate time each day to learning new words and their meanings. Use flashcards, vocabulary apps, or word-of-the-day calendars to enrich your lexicon.

One of the most effective ways to expand your vocabulary is through consistent and deliberate practice. By dedicating time each day to engage in vocabulary-building activities, you can gradually increase your word knowledge and enhance your language skills. There are various resources and tools available to aid you in this endeavor, including flashcards, vocabulary apps, and word-of-the-day calendars.

Flashcards have long been recognized as a valuable tool for vocabulary acquisition. They allow you to study words and their definitions in a structured and systematic manner, facilitating active recall and reinforcement of memory. Create flashcards for new words you encounter in your reading or daily life, and review them regularly to solidify your understanding and retention.

In addition to traditional flashcards, vocabulary apps offer a convenient and interactive way to learn new words. Many apps provide personalized quizzes, games, and exercises designed to help you learn and practice vocabulary in a fun and engaging way. Explore different vocabulary apps available on your smartphone or tablet, and find one that suits your learning style and preferences.

Another option for expanding your vocabulary is to subscribe to word-of-the-day calendars or newsletters. These resources deliver a new word and its definition to your inbox or calendar each day, exposing you to a diverse range of vocabulary and expanding your linguistic horizons. Incorporate these daily words into your vocabulary practice routine, and make an effort to use them in your writing and conversations to reinforce your learning.

By dedicating just a few minutes each day to learning new words and their meanings, you can gradually build a robust vocabulary that will serve you well in both written and spoken communication. Set aside time in your daily schedule for vocabulary practice, and make it a priority to engage consistently with your chosen learning methods. Over time, you will see significant improvement in your language skills and confidence in expressing yourself effectively.

8.2 Using Language in Context

Learning new words is just the first step; using them effectively in context is equally important. Practice incorporating newly learned words into your everyday conversations and writing, paying attention to context clues to reinforce understanding and usage.

Language is a dynamic and evolving entity, shaped by the interactions and experiences of its users. As you expand your vocabulary, it's crucial to actively engage with new words in real-world contexts to internalize their meanings and usage.

One effective strategy for incorporating new words into your vocabulary is to actively seek opportunities to use them in your everyday conversations. Whether you're chatting with friends, participating in discussions at work, or engaging in social interactions, make a conscious effort to integrate new words into your speech. Challenge yourself to find the right moments to introduce these words naturally, ensuring that they fit seamlessly into the flow of conversation. By actively using new words in context, you not only reinforce your understanding of their meanings but also develop confidence in your ability to use them effectively.

Similarly, practice incorporating newly learned words into your writing endeavors. Whether you're composing emails, essays, or creative projects, experiment with integrating new vocabulary into your prose. Pay attention to context clues and surrounding words to ensure that your usage is accurate and appropriate. Consider the tone and style of your writing, and tailor your language choices accordingly. By actively incorporating new words into your writing, you not only enhance your expressive capabilities but also deepen your understanding of how words function within different linguistic contexts.

By consistently practicing the integration of newly learned words into your conversations and writing, you reinforce their meanings and usage, making them an integral part of your expanding vocabulary. Embrace opportunities to engage with language in diverse contexts, and watch as your linguistic skills flourish.

Action Task: Practice incorporating newly learned words into your everyday conversations and writing. Pay attention to context clues to reinforce understanding and usage.

8.3 Exploring Language Through Reading

Reading is one of the most effective ways to expand your vocabulary and deepen your understanding of language. By immersing yourself in a wide range of texts across various genres and topics, you expose yourself to diverse vocabulary and language structures, enriching your linguistic knowledge and comprehension.

Reading serves as a gateway to the vast and varied landscape of language, offering endless opportunities for exploration and discovery. Whether you prefer fiction or nonfiction, novels or newspapers, poetry or prose, there's a wealth of material waiting to be explored.

To make the most of your reading experience, challenge yourself to read widely across different genres and topics. This exposure to diverse literary styles and subject matters not only broadens your horizons but also exposes you to a rich array of vocabulary and language structures.

As you delve into different texts, keep a journal of interesting words or phrases you encounter. Note down their definitions, contexts, and any other relevant information that will help you remember and understand them. By actively engaging with the language in this way, you reinforce your learning and make it easier to incorporate new words into your vocabulary.

Additionally, use your reading journal to track your progress and reflect on how your vocabulary has evolved over time. Celebrate your achievements and milestones, and use them as motivation to continue expanding your linguistic repertoire.

By immersing yourself in the rich tapestry of language through reading, you can not only expand your vocabulary and enhance your language skills but also develop a deeper appreciation for the power and beauty of words. So, grab a book, dive into a new world of language, and let the journey of discovery begin.

Action Task: Read widely across different genres and topics to expose yourself to diverse vocabulary and language structures. Keep a journal of interesting words or phrases you encounter, noting down their definitions and contexts. Use this journal to track your progress and reflect on your linguistic growth over time.

Chapter 9:
Practicing Regularly

In the journey to becoming a proficient speaker, consistent practice is paramount. This chapter delves into the importance of regular practice in honing speech skills, offering actionable tasks to integrate practice into daily life effectively. By establishing a routine, seeking feedback, and applying skills in real-world situations, individuals can cultivate confidence, clarity, and proficiency in their speaking abilities.

9.1 Making Speech Practice a Habit

Consistency is the cornerstone of skill development, and speech practice is no exception. To make meaningful progress in improving your speaking skills, it's essential to establish a regular practice routine. Whether you're working on articulation, pacing, or public speaking, dedicating consistent time and effort to practice is crucial.

Start by scheduling regular practice sessions in your calendar, just like you would for any other important commitment. Whether it's a daily 15-minute session or a weekly longer session, find a schedule that works for you and stick to it. Treat these practice sessions with the same level of importance and dedication as you would any other appointment or obligation.

During your practice sessions, focus on specific speech exercises tailored to your areas of improvement. This could include tongue twisters for articulation, vocal warm-ups for public speaking, or conversational practice for fluency. Experiment with different exercises and techniques to find what works best for you.

Consider practicing alone or with a partner, depending on your preferences and goals. Solo practice allows you to focus on individual skills and challenges, while practicing with a partner provides opportunities for feedback and interaction. Whichever approach you choose, make sure to stay committed and consistent in your practice efforts.

Remember, progress takes time and patience, so don't get discouraged if you don't see immediate results. Stay focused on your goals, stay consistent with your practice routine, and trust in the process. Over time, you'll see gradual improvement and development in your speaking skills.

Action Task: Schedule regular practice sessions for speech exercises, whether alone or with a partner. Consistency is key to improving your speaking skills.

9.2 Incorporating Feedback Loops

Feedback is a powerful tool for growth and improvement, providing valuable insights into areas of strength and areas for development. Incorporating feedback loops into your speech practice routine can help you identify areas of improvement, refine your skills, and track your progress over time.

Seek feedback from trusted sources, such as friends, family members, mentors, or language coaches, who can provide constructive criticism and guidance. Share your practice sessions with them and ask for their honest feedback on areas such as clarity, articulation, pacing, and overall delivery.

Be open-minded and receptive to feedback, even if it's constructive criticism. Remember that feedback is intended to help you improve, not to criticize or undermine your efforts. Take note of the feedback you receive and use it to adjust your practice routines accordingly.

Regularly review your goals and track your improvement over time. Keep a journal or log of your practice sessions, noting any areas of progress, challenges, or insights. Set specific benchmarks or milestones to work towards, and celebrate your achievements along the way.

Consider incorporating self-assessment tools into your practice routine, such as recording yourself speaking and reviewing the recordings for areas of improvement. This can provide valuable feedback and help you identify patterns or habits that may be hindering your progress.

By actively seeking feedback, adjusting your practice routines, and tracking your improvement over time, you can accelerate your progress and achieve your speaking goals more effectively.

Action Task: Seek feedback on your speaking progress from trusted sources and adjust your practice routines accordingly. Regularly review your goals and track your improvement over time.

9.3 Applying Skills in Real-Life Situations

Practice in controlled environments is essential for skill development, but real-life application is where you truly put your skills to the test. Look for opportunities to apply your newfound speaking skills in everyday situations, such as meetings, presentations, or social gatherings. The more you practice in real-life scenarios, the more confident and proficient you'll become.

Start by identifying situations or contexts where you can practice and apply your speaking skills. This could include leading a meeting at work, giving a presentation in class, participating in group discussions, or engaging in casual conversations with friends or colleagues. Be proactive in seeking out opportunities to speak and challenge yourself to step outside of your comfort zone.

When faced with speaking opportunities, apply the skills and techniques you've been practicing, such as clear articulation, confident delivery, and effective communication. Focus on engaging your audience, conveying your message with clarity and conviction, and responding adaptively to feedback or questions.

Don't be afraid to make mistakes or encounter challenges along the way. Embrace each speaking opportunity as a learning experience and an opportunity for growth. Reflect on your performance afterwards, identifying areas of strength and areas for improvement, and use this feedback to refine your skills for future occasions.

As you continue to apply your speaking skills in real-life situations, you'll gradually build confidence, competence, and credibility as a speaker. Each successful experience will reinforce your abilities and embolden you to tackle even more challenging speaking opportunities in the future.

By making speech practice a habit, seeking feedback to refine your skills, and applying your newfound abilities in real-life situations, you can cultivate confidence, competence, and mastery in your speaking skills. So, embrace every opportunity to speak, and watch as your confidence and proficiency soar.

Action Task: Look for opportunities to apply your newfound speaking skills in everyday situations, such as meetings, presentations, or social gatherings. The more you practice in real-life scenarios, the more confident you'll become.

Chapter 10:
Seeking Feedback and Improvement

Effective communication is a journey of continuous improvement, and seeking feedback is a crucial part of that journey. In this chapter, we will explore strategies for embracing constructive criticism, utilizing feedback for continuous improvement, and engaging in self-assessment and reflection to enhance your speaking skills.

10.1 Embracing Constructive Criticism

Constructive criticism is indeed a powerful catalyst for personal and professional development. When we shift our perspective from seeing feedback as criticism or judgment to viewing it as an opportunity for growth, we open ourselves up to a wealth of learning experiences.

By adopting a growth mindset, we recognize that feedback is not a reflection of our intrinsic value as individuals but rather an invaluable resource for honing our skills and reaching our full potential. Instead of feeling defensive or discouraged by feedback, we approach it with curiosity and openness, eager to glean insights that can help us improve.

In essence, a growth mindset empowers us to embrace feedback as a stepping stone on our journey toward mastery. Rather than viewing setbacks or areas for improvement as failures, we see them as valuable opportunities for learning and growth. This mindset fosters resilience, creativity, and a willingness to take risks, ultimately propelling us forward on our path to success.

So, the next time you receive constructive criticism, remember to embrace it with a growth mindset. Approach feedback as a gift rather than a burden, and use it as fuel to propel yourself toward your goals. With this mindset, you'll not only become a more effective communicator but also a more resilient and empowered individual.

Action Task: Develop a growth mindset by welcoming feedback as an opportunity for growth rather than criticism. Practice active listening and thank those who offer insights into your speaking.

To embrace constructive criticism effectively, practice active listening when receiving feedback. Listen attentively to the feedback provided, ask clarifying questions if necessary, and express gratitude to those who took the time to offer their insights. Remember that feedback is not a reflection of your worth as a person but rather an opportunity to identify areas for growth and development in your speaking skills.

10.2 Utilizing Feedback for Continuous Improvement

Absolutely! Constructive feedback becomes truly valuable when it serves as a catalyst for tangible improvements in our speaking skills. One effective way to ensure that feedback leads to meaningful progress is by establishing a feedback loop—an ongoing process of soliciting input, reflecting on insights, and incorporating suggested improvements into our practice routines.

The feedback loop begins with actively seeking input on our speaking from a variety of sources, including peers, mentors, or professionals. These individuals can offer valuable perspectives and insights that we may not have considered on our own. Whether it's feedback on vocal projection, articulation, or overall delivery, each observation provides an opportunity for growth.

Once we've gathered feedback, the next step is to reflect on the insights we've received and identify actionable areas for improvement. This may involve reviewing recordings of our speeches, analyzing audience reactions, or revisiting specific moments where feedback was given. By taking the time to reflect thoughtfully on the feedback we've received, we gain clarity on areas where we can focus our efforts for improvement.

The most critical aspect of the feedback loop is actively incorporating constructive feedback into our practice routines. This may involve adjusting our speech exercises, experimenting with new techniques, or seeking additional guidance from mentors or coaches. By integrating feedback into our practice sessions, we can refine our skills over time and track our progress toward our speaking goals.

The feedback loop is a dynamic and iterative process—it's not a one-time event but rather an ongoing cycle of learning and growth. By embracing this continuous feedback loop, we can harness the power of constructive criticism to continuously elevate our speaking skills and become more confident and effective communicators.

Action Task: Create a feedback loop by regularly soliciting input on your speaking from peers, mentors, or professionals. Actively incorporate constructive feedback into your practice routines.

To establish a feedback loop, seek out trusted individuals who can provide honest and constructive feedback on your speaking. This could include colleagues, friends, mentors, or professionals in the field of communication. Be specific about the areas you want feedback on, whether it's articulation, pacing, tone, or overall delivery. After receiving feedback, take time to reflect on the insights provided and identify actionable steps you can take to address areas for improvement in your practice sessions.

10.3 Self-Assessment and Reflection

Self-assessment and reflection are invaluable tools for personal growth and development, especially when it comes to honing our speaking skills. While external feedback provides valuable insights from others, self-assessment allows us to gain a deeper understanding of our own strengths, weaknesses, and areas for improvement. By setting aside time for introspection and reflection after speaking engagements, we can identify key takeaways, evaluate our performance, and develop strategies to enhance our speaking abilities moving forward.

One of the first steps in the process of self-assessment is to review and reflect on our recent speaking experiences. This may involve replaying recordings of our speeches, reviewing audience feedback, or simply recalling the details of the event. As we revisit these experiences, we can identify moments where we felt particularly confident or areas where we struggled. By pinpointing specific instances of success and areas for improvement, we can gain valuable insights into our speaking strengths and weaknesses.

Once we've identified areas for improvement, the next step is to develop strategies to address them in future practice sessions. This may involve setting specific goals for improvement, such as increasing vocal clarity, improving articulation, or enhancing overall delivery. By breaking down these goals into actionable steps, we can create a roadmap for our practice sessions and focus our efforts on areas that will have the most significant impact on our speaking skills.

During practice sessions, it's essential to be intentional about incorporating feedback from our self-assessment into our exercises and drills. For example, if we identify that we tend to rush through our speeches, we can focus on practicing pacing and taking deliberate pauses to allow for better audience comprehension.

Similarly, if we notice that our articulation could be clearer, we can incorporate tongue twisters and articulation exercises into our warm-up routine.

As we continue to practice and refine our speaking skills, it's essential to periodically revisit our self-assessment process to track our progress and reassess our goals. By regularly reflecting on our performance, identifying areas for improvement, and adjusting our practice strategies accordingly, we can ensure that we're continuously evolving and growing as speakers.

Ultimately, self-assessment and reflection are integral components of the journey toward mastery in speaking. By cultivating a habit of introspection and self-evaluation, we can become more self-aware, proactive, and intentional in our efforts to improve our speaking skills. Through consistent reflection and targeted practice, we can unlock our full potential as confident and effective communicators.

Action Task: Set aside time for self-reflection after speaking engagements. Identify areas of strength and areas for improvement, and develop strategies to address them in future practice sessions.

After speaking engagements, take time to reflect on your performance objectively. Identify aspects of your speaking that went well, such as clear articulation, engaging delivery, or effective use of body language. Also, pinpoint areas that may need improvement, such as pacing, vocal tone, or confidence level. Based on your self-assessment, develop specific strategies and exercises to target those areas in your future practice sessions.

By embracing constructive criticism, utilizing feedback for continuous improvement, and engaging in self-assessment and reflection, you can enhance your speaking skills and become a more confident and effective communicator.

Chapter 11:
Embracing Your Unique Voice

In a world where conformity often seems to be the norm, embracing your unique voice is a powerful act of self-expression and authenticity. Your voice is more than just the sound that emanates from your vocal cords; it's a reflection of your personality, experiences, and identity. In this chapter, we will explore the importance of celebrating individuality in speech, cultivating confidence in your voice, and finding your authentic speaking persona.

11.1 Celebrating Individuality in Speech

Each person's voice is a product of their individual journey through life, shaped by a myriad of influences ranging from cultural background to personal experiences. These factors converge to create a voice that is as unique as a fingerprint, distinct in tone, pitch, accent, and cadence. Rather than viewing these differences as shortcomings, they should be celebrated as expressions of individuality and diversity.

Take a moment to reflect on what makes your voice uniquely yours. Is it the warmth in your tone, the rhythm of your speech, or the inflections that punctuate your words? Perhaps it's the subtle nuances of your accent or the cadence that gives your speech its musicality. Whatever it may be, recognize that these qualities are what make your voice special and authentic.

Embracing your individuality as a strength rather than a weakness is essential in cultivating confidence and self-assurance in your communication. Instead of trying to conform to societal norms or emulate others, focus on being true to yourself and expressing your thoughts and ideas authentically. Your voice is a reflection of who you are as a person, and by embracing its uniqueness, you honor your identity and contribute to the richness of human expression.

Authenticity is a powerful force that resonates with others on a profound level. When you speak from the heart and allow your true self to shine through, you create a genuine connection with your audience that transcends superficialities. People are drawn to authenticity because it conveys sincerity, integrity, and vulnerability. By embracing your uniqueness and letting your voice be heard, you invite others to do the same, fostering deeper connections and understanding.

In a world that often values conformity over individuality, it takes courage to embrace the fullness of who you are and express yourself authentically. But the rewards of doing so are immeasurable. By celebrating your unique voice and allowing it to shine, you not only honor yourself but also inspire others to embrace their own authenticity. So, embrace your uniqueness, let your voice be heard, and celebrate the beauty of being true to yourself.

Action Task: Reflect on what makes your voice and speaking style unique. Embrace your individuality as a strength and focus on authenticity rather than conformity.

11.2 Cultivating Confidence in Your Voice

Confidence is indeed the linchpin that unlocks the full potential of your voice. It's the catalyst that propels you forward, commanding attention, exuding authority, and leaving an indelible mark on your audience. Cultivating confidence in your voice is not just about speaking louder or projecting more forcefully; it's about believing in yourself and embracing the inherent worth and value of your communication.

To cultivate confidence in your voice, start by adopting a mindset of self-belief and self-assurance. Recognize that you have something valuable to contribute to every conversation, presentation, or interaction, and approach each opportunity with a sense of conviction and purpose. Confidence is not about being flawless or having all the answers; it's about owning your voice and expressing yourself authentically and confidently, flaws and all.

One of the most effective ways to build confidence in your voice is through regular practice and rehearsal. Seek out opportunities to speak in front of others, whether it's volunteering to lead a meeting, participating in a public speaking club like Toastmasters, or simply engaging in conversations with friends and colleagues. The more you practice speaking, the more comfortable and confident you will become in your ability to communicate effectively.

Another crucial aspect of cultivating confidence in your voice is learning to silence your inner critic and banish self-doubt. Instead of dwelling on your perceived shortcomings or insecurities, focus on celebrating your strengths and unique qualities as a communicator. Recognize that your voice is valuable and worthy of being heard, and embrace the opportunity to share your thoughts and ideas with others.

Confidence in your voice is not something that happens overnight; it's a journey of self-discovery and self-empowerment. But with dedication, practice, and a positive mindset, you can cultivate the confidence you need to unleash the full power of your voice and make a lasting impact on those around you. So, speak up with confidence, knowing that your voice matters and has the power to inspire, influence, and ignite change.

Action Task: Practice speaking with conviction and passion, allowing your true personality to shine through. Remember that confidence in your voice comes from within.

11.3 Finding Your Speaking Persona

Finding your speaking persona is about discovering the speaking style that feels most authentic and comfortable for you. Just as actors adopt different personas when performing on stage, speakers can experiment with different speaking styles until they find one that resonates with their personality and values.

Start by exploring different aspects of your personality and how they manifest in your speech. Are you naturally outgoing and charismatic, or are you more reserved and introspective? Do you prefer to speak with humor and levity, or do you gravitate towards a more serious and contemplative tone?

Experiment with different speaking personas or styles to see which ones feel most authentic and comfortable for you. Try adopting a more formal or informal tone, varying your pacing and intonation, or incorporating storytelling and anecdotes into your speech. Pay attention to how each style aligns with your personality and values, and choose the one that feels most genuine to you.

Once you've found your speaking persona, embrace it wholeheartedly and allow it to guide your communication efforts. Remember that authenticity is key, so don't try to force yourself into a mold that doesn't feel right. Trust in your unique voice and speaking style, and let it shine through in all your interactions.

Action Task: Experiment with different speaking personas or styles until you find one that feels authentic and comfortable for you. Embrace the persona that best reflects your personality and values.

In conclusion, embracing your unique voice is a journey of self-discovery and self-expression. Celebrate your individuality, cultivate confidence in your voice, and find your authentic speaking persona. Remember that your voice has the power to inspire, influence, and impact others in profound ways. So speak up, speak out, and let your voice

Conclusion - A Journey of Healing

In conclusion, mastering the art of communication is a journey of self-discovery, growth, and empowerment. Throughout this guide, we've explored various aspects of effective communication, from building confidence and overcoming fears to refining pronunciation and embracing our unique voices.

We've learned that confidence is not an innate trait but a skill that can be cultivated through practice and perseverance. By adopting confidence-building practices and harnessing the power of strategic techniques such as power posing and visualization, we can expand our comfort zones and unlock our full potential as communicators.

We've also discovered the importance of clear pronunciation, breath control, vocal dynamics, and pacing in shaping the delivery and comprehension of our message. Through dedicated practice and attention to detail, we can strengthen our pronunciation skills, enhance vocal clarity, and captivate our audience with compelling delivery.

Furthermore, we've explored the significance of active listening, seeking feedback, and continuous improvement in honing our communication skills. By actively engaging with others, soliciting input, and reflecting on our performance, we can refine our abilities and strive for excellence in our communication endeavors.

Finally, we've emphasized the value of embracing our unique voices and speaking personas. By celebrating our individuality, cultivating confidence, and finding our authentic speaking style, we can connect more deeply with our audience and convey our message with authenticity and impact.

As we conclude this guide, let us remember that effective communication is not just about transmitting information but about fostering connection, understanding, and mutual respect. By embracing the principles and practices outlined in this guide, we can elevate our communication skills and make a positive impact in both our personal and professional lives. So, let us embark on this journey with confidence, curiosity, and a commitment to continuous growth and improvement.

Action Task: Reflect on your journey to improved speech fluency and confidence. Celebrate your progress and commit to continued growth and development in your speaking skills. Remember that fluency and confidence are lifelong pursuits that require dedication and perseverance. Keep practicing, keep learning, and keep speaking with clarity and conviction.

www.ingramcontent.com/pod-product-compliance
Lightning Source LLC
Chambersburg PA
CBHW050325230526
45471CB00005B/2356